Going Social
Ancient Secrets for Contemporary Relationships

Tony Wolfe, D.Ed.Min.
Foreword by Jim Richards

#GoingSocialBook

Dedication

This book is dedicated to my beautiful bride, Vanessa,
and my two wonderful sons, Ethan and Aaron.

CONTENTS

Foreword

by Jim Richards

I am privileged to have known Tony his whole life with the exception of the first few months. The first time I saw him I reached down and took him in my arms and held him. It has been surreal to now have him teach me eternal truth from the Bible. I welcome his mentoring. Let me share some thoughts about this great book, *Going Social*.

To begin with, everything in this book is saturated in the timeless truths of God's Word. Every chapter launches out from the foundation of Scripture. These Scriptural texts were written primarily by Israel's King Solomon, who is acclaimed as the wisest man who ever lived. What makes the writing so impactful is that God overshadowed the wording. God's Word always has value. Even if you are not a believer in Jesus Christ, your life on earth will be better if you live it by biblical guidelines. The biblical book of Proverbs is known as the book of wisdom. Read it to better relate to others.

Proverbs Chapter 18 is the basis for *Going Social*. Proverbs, in many cases, is a collection of pithy sayings. Often the subject matter jumps from one theme to another between verses. While Chapter 18 deals with interpersonal relationships, it covers a wide range of topics. This is helpful as we encounter various challenges along our respective paths.

Tony's transparency is a breath of fresh air. He uses personal stories to illustrate and apply the truths he communicates. Through his straight-forward approach, we are more comfortable to confront our own failings. Transparency is required in order to be a part of community. Tony helps us see who we are. We are flawed people because of Adam's nature. Every one of us stands in need of instruction, help and love. The chapters of this book point us to the tremendous need we all have.

Going Social is a blessing and a curse. We cannot cloister ourselves in monasteries to avoid contact with others. On the contrary, we are created to be social creatures. We are to interact for the benefit of others as well as for our own well-being. There are obstacles that often hinder us from going social. Tony deals with these truthfully, with grace. Once we do become a part of the human community there are pitfalls that can cause serious damage. We are susceptible to hurting ourselves and others. This is a risk we have to take because, realistically, there is no alternative.

One of the premises of the book is to teach us how to relate to others in a healthy way. This can be in personal conversation. It can be through electronic means. In today's culture, exponentially more people are using electronic devices to relate to others. But the disconnect is apparent. No one can experience a meaningful, fulfilling relationship from behind a screen. Yet, many social connections begin and flourish there. Eventually face-to-face connections must take place. Here, there can be no facades. Living social calls for a mutual accountability beyond a simple snapchat, tweet or post. Interaction in society puts us up close with certain interpersonal discomfort. We need one another, but we are fearful of rejection. Truly knowing someone is tricky, but the reward is well worth the risk.

For Christians this book raises to a new level the accountability we must have to one another. Believers who do life together in the community of the local church will rub against one another as nowhere else. Because the Word of God is clear, we have direction in caring for others. With the Holy Spirit's enablement we can live up to our social calling of being Christ's representatives on the earth. His priestly prayer for us in John Chapter 17 calls for us to be one even as He and the Father are one. This is a supernatural *Going Social.*

When we think of Going Social we often confine the image to some type of social media platform. Tony takes us beyond the limitations of these restraints. He is calling us to a Spirit-filled life that empowers us to contribute to those we love and to better society as a whole. How we act is important. How we react is even more important. The wisdom set forth in

Proverbs 18 is available for our enrichment. Take advantage of the insights of God's Word as explained and illustrated by Tony in this book. Once he was a child but now he has become a man, matured in God's Word. I challenge you to read and grow as you apply these ancient truths to your contemporary relationships.

Introduction

People are hard to love. I should know, because I am one. The world around you is full of real people who have real problems. They're not all bad though. There is love out there. Joy. Peace. Altruism. Kindness. But sometimes the good seems buried beneath compounded layers of nuisance or pain. Every person with whom you brush shoulders today has his or her own story. They are regretful over decisions made in the past, hopeful toward opportunities in the future and wrestling with life in the real world at the present. Jackie DeShannon took a shot at simplifying a solution to the psychosocial issues of our day: "What the word needs now / is love, sweet love / It's the only thing / that there's just too little of." Maybe she's right. Maybe genuine, Christlike love—"no, not just for some / but for everyone"—would make the world a much better place. But people are hard to love because they are real people with real problems. Just like me, and just like you. But living in healthy, meaningful community is not beyond you. It is well within your reach.

Have you considered how much easier it is to engage in social interaction today than it ever has been before? In 1928 the first television broadcast was transmitted between London and New York. Television broadcast stations were soon established and families began to sit around the box of moving pictures daily. The television brought both instant information and instant entertainment from thousands of miles away into the home. By 1950 there were 98 commercial television stations on the air in the United States. By 2017 that number had grown to 1,761. We would all agree that television is not today what it was back then, and that it invites a certain set of dangers into the home of the unwise and undiscerning. But the world of television is still a constant source of cultural saturation in the American home. Children, adolescents, adults and senior adults all learn social behaviors and global happenings from the comfort of their own couches. For decades, television programming has been both a reflection of the culture and a driving factor from within it.

In 1969 the first successful transmission of information was made through an internet network called "ARPANET" from the University of California in Los Angeles to Stanford Research Institute. When I was in Junior High School in Baton Rouge, Louisiana, I remember doing research in our library for a science project. I pulled out the trusty old Encyclopedia Britannica from the shelf and turned to the C's to look for "computer." However, the particular set of encyclopedias our school's library shelved was printed in 1969, and "computer" was not even a word at that time. We did not have an actual computer in our home until the mid 1990's, and even then it was not much like the machine sitting beneath my fingertips as I type this introduction. Oregon Trail and Solitaire were about the only things it was good for, except dial-up internet so I could check my paid AOL email account (which I still have today—don't judge me). Today, 80% of American households have at least one desktop or laptop computer and 84% of American households have at least one handheld smart device such as a smartphone or tablet.

The first social media platform, Six Degrees, was created on the internet in 1997. The first blogging sites became popular two years later. Through the early 2000's, MySpace, LinkedIn, Flicker, YouTube and others began to take shape and to redefine the rules of social interaction in our generation. On February 4, 2004 in Cambridge, Massachusetts college student Mark Zuckerberg and his roommates launched a new kind of social media connection platform they called Facebook. In March of 2006, Twitter went live at the hands of Jack Dorsey and three friends. As I write these words, Facebook currently has 2.19 billion active profiles and Twitter boasts 336 million active users every month. Social media has become both the standard of online interaction and the number one driving factor for cyber-social interface in the postmodern world.

Over the last several decades the globalization of the Western mind has been boosted by television, internet, social media and other rapidly advancing technology. The whole world is at your fingertips. Only three decades ago our culture defined social interaction in terms of the small group of face-to-face friends with whom one could regularly keep up. Today, we have added on top of this the maximum number of connections, friends and followers our social media platforms will allow. Not only is the world at our fingertips, but an instant audience is at our fingertips as well. Every "like" or "share" does something psychologically to the one who posts a thought. The short bursts of approving comments, hearts and "preach it" GIF's give affirmation to every publicized opinion and conviction. Every user becomes an expert and every expert has an instant audience.

One would think that expanded social interface has increased our ability to interact in a healthy manner. On the contrary, the opposite has become true. Because human beings are social creatures deeply wounded by the effects of a world scarred by sin, life together (both in person and online) is complicated by the reality of impassioned interpersonal disagreements. As our social circles expand, our platforms for opinion-staking and judgment-casting also expand.

On our social media accounts we get to choose who listens to us and to whom we listen. We can easily create our own little cyber-social world where our opinions and convictions are always affirmed and never substantially challenged. If you think this self-serving, introspective psychosocial tendency stays within the realm of our online connections, you're wrong. Our face-to-face interactions quickly begin to mimic the prideful introspection of our online propensities. Ten years ago we said that a cantankerous, divisive person could "hide behind the keyboard." Today, they do not feel the need. If we can say sharp, egotistical words with no consequences among our online friendships amassing to ourselves those who will only agree with us, we can do so face-to-face as well. And if the expectation online is that we either agree with our friends' posted opinions or keep silent, the expectation is the same face-to-face as well. So healthy disagreement in our social circles is bankrupted by intellectual, theological, political and philosophical social relativism. The need for ancient wisdom in contemporary social life has never been greater.

This book does not come from the culmination of a few months' work. Rather, it comes from the reflection of three and a half decades of experiences, failures, victories, interactions and observations. I pray that as you work through its chapters you will do so prayerfully and self-reflectively. While many of the examples and applications contained in these pages are based on my own research or observations, the truths they demonstrate belong to Someone infinitely wiser and more experienced than me. Allow me to communicate several concessions that may help you understand my own presuppositions and convictions as you begin your journey through this book.

ONE: The truth contained in this book belongs uniquely to the God of the Bible. He owns the rights to everything true and wise you will read in the next twenty-four chapters. Sure there are experiences, evidences and applications shared from the timeline of human history, including some from my own timeline. But ultimately, everything that is true in these pages belongs to the timeless God of the Ages. I believe that the Bible in its sixty-six books is the inspired, inerrant, infallible and authoritative Word of the Living God. The Holy Spirit literally breathed out the words of God through the mouths and fingers of men in such a way that he preserved their particular writing styles and personality idiosyncrasies while using their words to communicate eternal truths that were, and always will be, beyond themselves. As you read and apply the wisdom contained in these twenty-four chapters, please understand that 100% of what is true and trustworthy belongs to God.

TWO: This book is not only for Christians. Although the wisdom contained in these pages is straight from the Bible, this is not one of those Christian-only books. Whether you believe in the God of the Bible or not, the biblical principles of wisdom between the covers of *Going Social: Ancient Wisdom for Contemporary Relationships* promises to make a huge difference in your life when it comes to developing and maintaining healthy relationships. The biblical text is made up of many different kinds of literary genres. There are books comprised mostly of historical narrative (ie: Genesis, Exodus, Acts), beautiful poetry (ie: Psalms, Song of Solomon), personal and pastoral letters (Galatians, Ephesians, Philemon) apocalyptic literature (Revelation and parts of Daniel and Ezekiel) wisdom literature (ie: Proverbs, Ecclesiastes) and more. *Going Social* deals with Proverbs Chapter 18, which is wisdom literature. The nature of wisdom literature is that these are wise sayings that are based on the way God has designed the world to work. The sayings are not necessarily promises of God, but rather most common occurrences. In other words, wise sayings are designed to be proven accurate nine times out of ten, no matter who you are or what you believe. So the principles of true wisdom apply to you no matter who you are. My challenge to non-Christians readers would be this: When you learn and practice the biblical principles contained in this book, give serious consideration to the fact that the God who revealed this timeless wisdom has also revealed himself to you in the entirety of the Bible's pages. Let this be a point of entrance for you into the wonders of the biblical text. If you find the biblical wisdom useful and true, dig in even more to the rest of God's Word as well and watch how God will speak to you through it.

THREE: The most important information is contained in the Afterword. Yep, right here at the beginning I'm telling you the best thing about this book is at its end. The Afterword explains the message to salvation outlined in the pages of the Bible. The Afterword is good news. It's the best news. As helpful as biblical, proverbial wisdom on relationships is to someone who is a non-Christian, if your horizontal relationships (with other people) are made healthier while your vertical relationship (with God) is neglected, the benefit you receive from biblical wisdom will be short-lived. Although non-Christians will gain mounds of wisdom from these pages, apart from a relationship with God through repentance from sin and faith in Jesus Christ everything herein amounts to nothing more than a temporary fix to an eternal problem. Whoever you are and whatever walk of life you come from, God loves you with a relentless love. You have been created in his image and after his likeness. You are beautiful by design and designed for a beautiful purpose. For more about how to have an eternity-changing relationship with the God who created you, see the Afterword.

I find it necessary, also, to share briefly about my own journey in writing this book. This began as an exercise of my personal daily quiet time with the Lord. For twenty-four days straight I decided to focus on one verse per day in Proverbs Chapter 18, which seemed to have a great deal to say about my life with others. Every morning I got up, fixed myself a cup of coffee, took the dog outside in the back yard and sat down at the back porch table. I would read the verse, hand-copy it in my journal and memorize it, repeating it to myself several times. When I felt like I had the verse memorized I began to journal. I committed to writing one full page in my personal journal with the first thoughts that came to my mind as I meditated on the particular verse for the day. When the page was full, I stopped and read back through what I had written, making no changes.

Then, at the bottom of the page I would write myself a short, one to three sentence prayer asking the Lord for the grace to apply the verse in real time.

For the reader's benefit I have included the prayers I wrote for myself as well as single-page space for you to journal your own thoughts, as I did, as you meditate on each verse (one verse per chapter in *Going Social*) of Proverbs Chapter 18. This is not necessary, but it is a great option. You can turn this contemporary commentary into a life-transforming personal journaling experience if you'll just set aside 20-30 minutes a day for the next 24 days.

As I read, memorized, meditated on and prayed over each verse for 30 minutes in the mornings, something amazing happened. The verse stayed with me all day long. While I was driving, eating lunch, writing emails or dialoguing with friends the verse for the day kept popping into my mind. This proved to be a good thing for me. As it turned out, the Lord gave me opportunities to put into practice exactly what I had prayed each day. It would take too long to share all the stories. But sometimes, seriously, I was blown away when the moment popped up for me to practice what I had prayed that morning.

I'm willing to bet that if you spend the time meditating on, journaling about and praying through these verses of ancient wisdom, God will give you daily opportunities to put them into practice as well. When that happens, write your stories down so that at a future date you can go back and remember what God has shown you and taught you.

The point of this book is to help you—and me—develop and maintain healthy relationships at home, at work, among friends and online. I have not sought to add to or manipulate the truth of Proverbs Chapter 18 at all. Rather, my goal has been to expose this ancient wisdom faithfully while paving smooth pathways toward contemporary application. I pray that the truth of God's Word is faithfully represented and its timely application builds a foundation for healthy interaction in all of your social circles. This is nothing new. It has been around for thousands of years. This is ancient wisdom for contemporary relationships. As you dig in, let this wisdom of old produce hope anew in all of your dealings with real people who have real problems, just like you.

1. Go Social

"One who isolates himself pursues selfish desires;
he rebels against all sound wisdom."
Proverbs 18:1

Simon and Garfunkle weave their lyrical magic: "I've built walls / a fortress deep and mighty / that none may penetrate / I have no need of friendship / friendship causes pain / it's laughter and it's loving I disdain / I am a rock / I am an island." Even as a young boy these words resonated with me. People are crazy and complicated. I should know because I am one. It seems an appealing fantasy to just lock ourselves away where we don't have to deal with anyone else. I have my own problems. And the more people I have to deal with, the more those problems compound. If I could just pretend like no one else exists, surely life would be better.

This sounds dumb but there was a time in my childhood when I literally thought everyone besides me must be some kind of robot. All the emotions I had, thoughts I entertained, places I was going and plans I had made—there's no way billions of upright anthropoids wrapped in flesh could have those same daily experiences. So I built this psychosomatic fortress around my own ego. Perhaps you have done this in some way, too. I guess you could say I was in my own little world. I felt safe there—free from the possibility that the lives of others might be as significant or as valuable as my own. It did not take long, however, to realize just how lonely and meaningless that little world truly is.

At the time of my writing, more than one billion people are active on Facebook. More than one-hundred million are active on Instagram and over three-hundred-and-thirty million are active on Twitter monthly. One-hundred-fifty-eight million use Snapchat every day, opening the app eighteen times from sun up to sun down. Social media is a new norm in the Twenty-First Century. Taking your social life online is not necessarily a bad thing, but it is certainly not the main thing. Social media can be a blessing and it can also be a curse.

It is said that only seven percent of what we communicate is made up of the actual words we choose. The other ninety-three percent comes from our facial expressions, tone and inflection of voice, body language, history with the individual, emotions at the moment, and more. Recognizing this, social media gurus have enhanced their platforms with emojis, GIF's, color and font options and instant "disappearing" shares of personal videos, audio clips, and pictures (just so you know, nothing you post online ever actually disappears). But still, there is a potentially unhealthy disconnect from the real world while socializing from behind a keyboard or a cell phone.

Have you noticed that people are often more likely to say something controversial or degrading when they say it on social media than they would if saying it in person? Think through the number of Twitter accounts and blog profiles that are created in anonymity, not revealing the user's true identity, for the sole purpose of saying things boldly and brashly. Now think through how many of those accounts you follow, on purpose. We like the idea of speaking our minds without consequences, and of agreeing with others who speak our minds without accountability.

But this book is not about social media alone. It's about community. God created humankind with an inherent longing for—need for—community. After naming the animals in Genesis Chapter 2, Adam looked around at all that was created and saw that there was no one like him with whom to share his life. "It is not good," said the Creator, " for the man to be alone." Millennia later, it is still not good for man to be alone. Aloneness does not mean incompleteness. But aloneness does tend to lead toward selfishness. The wise, ancient king wrote, "One who isolates himself pursues selfish desires." When we live in our own little worlds—whether physically or emotionally—self-gratification is the only standard for truth. There exists nothing to pursue except what promises personal satisfaction. We become our own gods, our own judges and our own juries. Isolation is not a solution for life's frustrations. Sure, it is a good idea to pull away once in a while to regroup and to give yourself room to think. But no one should live in perpetual isolation. It's just not healthy. It's not human.

Do you remember Tom Hanks in the movie *Cast Away*? The movie netted almost 29 million dollars on its USA opening weekend alone in December of 2000. For some of us, being stranded on our own island in the middle of a beautiful, vast ocean sounds like a dream come true. No one to argue with. No one to discourage or annoy us. After all, "a rock feels no pain / and an island never cries." But after only a few days, Chuck (Tom Hanks' character) started to feel the effects of isolation. The movie climaxes to a heart-wrenching scene where Chuck's only friend in the world— Wilson, a volleyball on which he has drawn facial features—floats away never to be found again. Chuck's inherent longing for community, while isolated from the rest of the world, literally drove him insane. Isolation left him to pursue only those desires for which he felt a sense of immediacy, for his own good. And deep down he found that what was immediately necessary for his own good was something he could never find in isolation. He needed community. He needed to go social. Sure, community brings its own set of problems. But emotional or physical isolation robs us of the joys of sharing, caring, empathy and fellowship.

But that's not all. Ancient proverbial wisdom informs us that one who isolates himself also "rebels against all sound wisdom." One benefit of going social is that we get to learn from the collective wisdom of our community—both past and present. But when we isolate ourselves we cannot possibly learn from the mistakes or successes of either our ancestors or our contemporaries. Rebelling against all sound wisdom is equivalent to living a fool. It is not only unhealthy, but altogether foolish to reject community. Without others around me speaking into my life, I am much less likely to see my own foolishness or to recognize my own pitfalls.

Living in purposeful community requires a level of trust and openness. It is possible to be physically communal without being emotionally communal: a well-polished outer shell concealing the secret anxieties of a conflicted spirit. It is not enough to just be around people. We need to be with people—even the ones we do not like. As J.R. Tolkien's Bilbo Baggins so eloquently stated to his companions in *The Fellowship of the Ring*, "I don't know half of you half as well as I should like; and I like less than half of you half as well as you deserve." But the journey they would take together produced something inside of Bilbo Baggins that he never could have expected to find on his own. "Adventure" was not just something he found in personal courage, but in collective fellowship. This fellowship was not really about a ring. It was about a journey of friendship, wisdom, trust, struggle and hope.

It is not just unhealthy to live in isolation. It is altogether foolish. The insulated narcissist pursues only the selfish moment yet finds no meaningful satisfaction in anything he finds. The one who embraces meaningful community pursues what gives way to wisdom and finds the satisfaction of the journey through all that he endures.

The first step to going social is to do just that. You can do this. Invest yourself in more than yourself. Pursue meaningful community. Go social.

PRAYER

Lord, keep me from the false satisfaction of physical and emotional isolation. Give me community to enjoy and to embrace. Teach me to love accountability and to listen to and learn from the wisdom of others. Help me to live in the freedom of community instead of in the isolation of rebellion.

JOURNAL

_____

_____

_____

_____

_____

_____

_____

_____

_____

_____

_____

_____

_____

_____

_____

_____

_____

_____

_____

_____

_____

_____

_____

_____

_____

_____

_____

_____

_____

_____

GOING SOCIAL

2. Listen for Understanding

"A fool does not delight in understanding,
but only wants to show off his opinions."
Proverbs 18:2

It was dark and I was tired. Maybe that will warrant a bit of sympathy with my reader. I was driving in downtown Houston (for Texas readers, perhaps this will warrant even more sympathy). I sat motionless waiting for the arrow to turn green, my mind in a million different places. I have that tendency, to sometimes get lost in deep thought and put physical motions on autopilot. It's not healthy. I know. I'm working on it. But on this particular night I saw the arrow turn green, signaling permission to make the turn. Mindlessly, I put gentle pressure on the accelerator, spun the wheel counterclockwise and proceeded down the blacktop. Only a few seconds later the solitude of my deep thought was effectively interrupted by the sound of honking horns, the sight of flashing headlights and a couple of single-fingered hand waves. "What's their problem?" I thought. Until I realized that I was going the wrong way down a divided highway. On each side of the median, the sign said vehicles are allowed to go only one way. In my defense, I was only going one way. It just happened to be the wrong way.

Communication is a two-way street. If you are so lost in your own thoughts that you cannot listen to or understand what others around you are trying to get across, there is danger ahead. Ignore the warning signs and you are headed for disaster. You can argue your point your way all day. But if it's always your way or the highway, you'll find yourself on a dangerous roadway all day every day. In order to effectively communicate, someone has to be picking up what you're laying down and you've got to be picking up what others are laying down. Otherwise there is no exchange, only loss.

"A fool does not delight in understanding," writes the king in words of ancient wisdom, "but only wants to show off his opinions." Something that delights you is something that brings you joy and gladness of heart. It is something you pursue, something you desire. One who is wise delights in understanding. He wants to hear, to listen, and to comprehend. When someone else is speaking, his full attention is devoted to understanding not just words and sentences, but also the emotions, thoughts and intentions that lay behind them.

This is particularly difficult in heated conversations. As a rule of thumb, the most offended party is to speak first since offense has a tendency to cloud the mind and callous the heart—more on this in Chapter 19. Conversations between the wise progress healthily as one party speaks and the other listens for understanding. Conversely, exchanges between the foolish escalate quickly as both parties speak while neither listens for understanding. Here is a good rule of thumb, from ancient wisdom: seek to understand before you seek to be understood. Hang on every word. Pick up on non-verbal communication. Offer your full attention. Delight in understanding.

Even in cordial conversations, the same principles apply. There is great fulfillment in coming to understand someone—to know them. Most people love to talk about themselves. Learn to listen more than you talk. If your goal in entering a conversation is to show off what you know or what you think, this is a foolish pursuit.

Is it more important to you—more delightful for you—that others know how you think and feel or that you know how others think and feel? While others are speaking to you are you formulating a response in your mind, or are you diligently processing what they say and why they say it?

When a mature gorilla is challenged by a younger gorilla, he beats his chest and screams at the top of his lungs. It's a primitive show-off routine designed to humiliate the weaker of the two while proving alpha status. It gets very loud very quickly. There's a lot of vocalization, but not much is actually communicated. When we show off our opinions, we are no different. Two parties beating their chests and escalating the volume never communicate anything. They might eventually come to a mutual understanding, but neither has actually understood the other. There's a lot of vocalization, but not much is actually communicated. When communication becomes competition, we've lost the whole point of the matter. We've stopped trying to understand the other and have resorted to just beating our chests to prove dominance.

Come to think of it, showing off anything is a rather foolish pursuit. Whatever one has he only possesses by the grace of God. This includes any measure of intellect, perspective or knowledge. There is no such thing as a self-made man. The very air we breathe is a gift to us from God. Moreover, we all are who we are on the shoulders of those who have gone before us. The temptation to show off an opinion is deeply rooted in selfish pride. And selfish pride is a delusional illness—a hallucinative drug.

Wherever opinions are elevated facts are ignored. Opinions are often emotionally charged and circumstantially formulated. Facts do not bend to convincing arguments to their contrary. Instead, they remain unchanged and unmoved. "Facts are stubborn things," wrote the second president of the United States, "and whatever may be our wishes, our inclinations, or the dictates of our passions, they cannot alter the state of facts and evidence." Only a fool would allow his passions, wishes, and inclinations to convince his mind of something that is contrary to reality. Only a fool would belligerently stand on that opinion with no desire to appreciate his opposition. Only a fool would boast an opinion that is divorced from understanding.

We live in a culture that often rejects understanding altogether. We have lost the art of disagreeing civilly, having replaced it with the tendency to develop and disseminate immediate opinions, with or without facts. On social media we unfriend and/or block those who do not share our opinions. In public we isolate ourselves from them. We prefer the stagnant, shallow waters of mindless cliques over the beautiful, cascading waterfalls of true community. We do not delight in understanding our opposing parties. Instead, we gather to ourselves those who will listen to and affirm our expressed opinions.

I am always hesitant to enter a restaurant that boasts of its own greatness: "The Best BBQ in Texas," or "Louisiana's Finest Creole Kitchen." The greatest does not have to tell others of its greatness. If your conversations are full of self-promotion, boasting your own opinions and supreme wisdom while absent diligent listening and sincere understanding, foolishness is your only friend. You are headed the wrong way down a one-way street, and nothing but disaster lies ahead.

Start picking up what others are laying down. Start valuing the viewpoint of your opposition before formulating and boasting your own opinions. When someone is speaking, give them your full attention. Don't settle for simply hearing. Listen with diligent effort. Effective communication is crucial to going social. And it is impossible without a sincere commitment to understanding.

PRAYER

Father in Heaven, when my opinions are strong give me the self-control to listen for understanding. When my viewpoint is challenged, make me a lover of the truth. Give me the discipline to listen to others and seek to understand them. Guard me from my own arrogance.

JOURNAL

_____

_____

_____

_____

_____

_____

_____

_____

_____

_____

_____

_____

_____

_____

_____

_____

_____

_____

_____

_____

_____

_____

_____

_____

_____

_____

_____

_____

3. Search Your Heart

"When a wicked person comes, contempt also comes,
and along with dishonor, derision."
Proverbs 18:3

Remember when good was good and bad was bad? I know. That's so cliché these days. I remember watching *The Wizard of Oz* when I was a kid growing up in South Louisiana. The powerful contrast between black-and-white and color in the film captivated its audience. Good and evil were clearly defined and characters were unmistakably of one persuasion or the other. True to the rising influence of postmodernism, in 1995 Gregory Maguire wrote a spin off on the classic entitled *Wicked: The Life and Times of the Wicked Witch of the West*. (Interestingly, two years later Gus Van Sant's 1997 film *Good Will Hunting* contains perhaps the first public usage of the word "wicked" to be slang for "good" or "awesome").

In May of 2003, a Broadway Musical debuted based on Maguire's version of the Oz narrative. *Wicked* quickly became the most popular musical on Broadway. Still today it is often referred to as "Broadway's biggest blockbuster." In *Wicked*, Elphaba (the Wicked Witch of the West) is painted both wicked and green as a victim of circumstances beyond her control: conceived illegitimately, mistreated by her father, separated from her sister, tricked by her roommate, disillusioned by an ill-fated love interest, and labeled a rebel against the unethical government of Oz. In Maguire's tale, the Wicked Witch of the West wasn't really that wicked at all. At least, not when compared to the wickedness of the society that gave her such a misguided and undeserved label.

In the nineteen-sixties, American professor and philosopher Joseph Fletcher founded and taught his theory of social ethics, claiming that the collective good of a society defined the right and wrong of each individual. This shifted standards of good and bad, right and wrong, from unchanging criteria anchored in timeless truth to the shifting tides of social constructivism relative to each culture and generation.

Today, our culture has gone one step further blurring lines between wickedness and righteousness, good and bad. Truth has become relative altogether and right/wrong are the prerogative of each individual. "My truth," and "your truth," we hear. The only standard of truth is what I think and how I feel. Labeling someone wicked or bad based on their actions is incompatible with moral relativism. Wickedness is a construct of uneducated or unenlightened myths, we suppose. By our standards, even the Boomers' and Gen-Xers' archetypal embodiment of wickedness, the Wicked Witch of the West, is not really that wicked at all.

But according to ancient truth, wickedness is not a social construct. It is a condition of the heart. Consider the words of Augustine, Bishop of Hippo between 396-430 AD: "I inquired what wickedness is, and I didn't find a substance, but a perversity of will twisted away from the highest substance – You oh God – towards inferior things, rejecting its own inner life and swelling with external matter." Ancient truth places wickedness and righteousness on opposite ends of the social spectrum. Wickedness is a choice of action rooted in a disease of the heart.

King Solomon has employed poetic parallelism here; he has written the same thing twice, only using different words. "When a wicked person comes, contempt also comes, and along with dishonor, derision." Wickedness, contempt, dishonor, and derision are all cut from the same cloth. Notice the wise king is not focusing on the actions of the individual, but the condition. The identity. The person is wicked and therefore does wicked things. Wickedness here is not an occasional act of the hands. It is a condition of the heart.

There are those, in going social, whose very presence elevates the environment and lifts the spirit. I'm thinking of a friend of mine who lives not far from where I work. When he walks into the office to say hello, he announces his presence with some uplifting phrase like, "Well Amen! How are my favorite people today?" Or "I'm telling you what, I'm just so blessed I can hardly stand it!" He is not being patronizing or unrealistic. Rather, humbled sincerity is evident in every word. He can enter the most anxious of situations and diffuse tension with a single word. He is a righteous man and with his presence always come encouragement, joy, peace and inspiration. His heart is pure and purity follows him wherever he goes.

There are others, in going social, whose very presence can wilt the living plants in a room. Their facial expressions, tone of voice, and choice of conversational content all reek of death and despair. They complain about everything, accuse about anything and care about nothing. Except maybe themselves. Their hearts are calloused by pride, hard as stones. Every word is laced with malevolence and every conversational contribution stained with spite. When they open their mouths conversations turn from contentment to contempt, from grace to gossip, from edification to evil, from dignity to derision. Their hearts are wicked, and wickedness follows wherever they go.

What are the majority of your conversations like? Do you often find yourself in contemptuous conversations? Across the spectrum of your relationships among family, friends and coworkers, are your conversations mostly contentious or mostly encouraging? If there is a common equation across all of your social circles, there is also a common denominator. Perhaps that common denominator is you. The only way to solve the equations of your social circles differently is to change the common denominator. You can't change other people. But you can change you.

Search your heart and ask, "What is it I am hoping to get out of this conversation?" If the answer is more about you than it is about the other person(s), you may need to start by evaluating your heart instead of your social equations. Wickedness always promotes self. Righteousness always elevates others. Living in community is about enjoying the presence of others and valuing what they bring to the table. A wicked heart seeks to divide, to destroy and to devastate. A righteous heart seeks to engage, to encourage and to enjoy.

I have no doubt the Wicked Witch of the West's upbringing, had this been a true story, would prove a difficult set of circumstances for her to overcome. But in searching your heart, this truth remains consistent through the ages: your emotions are your responsibility. Search your heart and you will find that it is true. Contemporary history is replete with examples of men and women who have overcome adverse circumstances, social exclusion and ill-fated dreams to become gracious, conscientious members of society. Going social is dangerous when we have allowed adverse circumstances to infect our hearts with the disease of wickedness. But it is a gift to the world when our hearts are pure with righteousness and full of grace.

The good news is that the Inspiration behind Proverbs 18:3 is also the Inspiration behind Ezekiel 36:26. "I will give you a new heart and put a new spirit within you," declares the very giver of life. If you have searched deeply and are convicted about the condition of your heart, I invite you to read through the Afterword before returning to Chapter 4.

PRAYER

Lord Jesus, search my heart and know me. Reveal to me the wickedness in my own heart and remove it with your righteous hand. Keep me from the wicked whenever possible. And make my speech wholesome, pure and edifying in every situation.

JOURNAL

_____
_____
_____
_____
_____
_____
_____
_____
_____
_____
_____
_____
_____
_____
_____
_____
_____
_____
_____
_____
_____
_____
_____
_____
_____
_____
_____
_____
_____
_____
_____

4. Test the Waters

"The words of a person's mouth are deep waters,
a flowing river, a fountain of wisdom."
Proverbs 18:4

My boys and I love to watch Jeremy Wade's *River Monsters*. We sit on the couch, popcorn and sweet tea in hand, living vicariously through his exciting angling expeditions. A few days ago we watched the episode, again, in which he was attempting to discover the secret of the United Kingdom's legendary Loch Ness Monster. Early in the episode he put on his wet suit, strapped snorkeling gear to his face and dove into the murky water to explore. From the shoreline he followed the contour of the lake's bottom from one foot to ten feet. From fifteen feet to twenty-five feet. And then with little warning the bottom of the lake plunged into urgent, abysmal darkness. The camera panned out to show the dramatic effect of the watery depths. Seven-hundred feet of deep, dark secrets. If there was a monster living in that lake, no one would ever see it in its natural habitat with the naked eye. If it had ever come to the surface in Loch Ness, it came from deep, dark, secret places no one could begin to fathom. What kind of monster could possibly live down there? What would it eat? What would it look like? All questions that have teased the imaginations of fishermen and vessel captains for over fifteen-hundred years.

Communication is a wonderful gift from God. Have you stopped lately to contemplate how amazing it is that human beings can formulate consonant and vowel sounds in such a way that their vocalization produces successful representation of something tangible, abstract or emotive? That upon hearing these simple vocalized patterns the listener can gain insight into the speaker's thoughts and heart? That those whose biology does not permit them to vocalize or to hear vocalizations can communicate to the same extent using signals of the hand or strokes on a page? Where does this come from? From the deep, dark places of our hearts. Words, phrases, sentences, paragraphs and dissertations all flow from the deep waters of one's innermost being.

I am convinced that as far as Loch Ness is concerned, no monster truly lives there. You may believe in a lurking monster beneath those watery depths, but I think what people see there are either figments of their imagination or can be naturally explained by something tangible, yet unexpected.

Concerning righteous communicators, while the depths of the spirit are vast, by the grace of God no monster lives there. Deep doesn't always mean dangerous. The wisdom gained from such speech is drawn from the depths of a pure heart. And this wisdom always brings grace and peace to the hearer. Concerning wicked communicators, however, monsters have made their homes in the deep recesses of the dark and secret. They surface with every word spoken or key struck. Wisdom gained from such speech is the wisdom of caution. Keep a safe distance and carefully marvel at the conspicuous revulsions of a social leviathan. Going social can be daunting because you never know what monsters may surface from the depths of your heart or from the hearts of another.

In the words of the greatest Communicator who ever lived, the very *logos* of God himself, "From the overflow of the heart the mouth speaks," (Luke 6:45). Even when our words are spontaneous or emotionally charged, they are drawn from the wellspring of our hearts. The fountain of communicative wisdom is a water-well drilled deeply into the spirit of a man. Whether carefully drawn out or carelessly spilled over, every word is fetched from the same well. Any way you look at it, what is coming out of the mouth is coming from the depths of the heart. To test the heart, test the waters.

The *River Monsters* episode recalled efforts of marine biologists in recent years to comb the watery depths using sonar technology, hoping to once-and-for-all either prove the loch's great legend or put it to bed. This lengthy process synchronizing dozens of ships produced a detailed topographical picture of the loch's bottom (but as far as we know, no monster).

Notice the "flowing river" that comes from a person's mouth in King Solomon's proverb and think of it as social sonar, painting a picture of the depths of our hearts over a period of time. The words we say over time give an accurate topographical picture of the watery depths of our hearts. What comes up from the bottom is seen over time on the top. Eventually, if you listen for understanding, the deep dark recesses of a person's heart are revealed through what they say, what they don't say, and how/when they say what they say. To test the heart, test the waters.

What if you were to take a social sonar of your own communication? What might be revealed from the watery depths of your heart? Do you expend most of your breath speaking about a particular topic, desire or problem? What percentage of your conversations is encouraging and uplifting? What percentage is crude, facetious or unhealthy? What are the words of your mouth revealing about the hidden contours of your heart?

What a blessing it is when cascading waters pour from the storehouse of Godly wisdom! How regretful when the only wisdom gleaned from one's words is the caution for others to steer clear. How embarrassing when God searches the depths of our hearts only to find elusive, shameful monsters lurking there.

Since I was a boy I have enjoyed swimming in rivers and lakes. My wife, not so much. Just about the only test I perform before I jump in is the toe-test. You know, to make sure the water is warm enough. Vanessa, however, gets online to check the mercury levels, the history of toxic waste dumps and news articles reporting cases of recent parasitic or bacterial contaminations. We both test the water, I guess. But her tests are much more exhaustive than mine.

Perhaps the next time you consider jumping into the moving stream of a conversation, you should test the waters. Is this conversation healthy? Is it sincere? Is it edifying or demeaning? Is speaking into this conversation a good thing to do? By simply listening, am I complicit with some manner of unrighteousness? Are there any social parasites lurking around to jump in at the right moment and turn something questionable into something disastrous? Are the waters infected with surreptitious social bacteria, slowly eating away at all that is good about the conversation? Don't jump in before you test the waters.

What comes out of the mouth is always germinated in the heart. The heart of a man is deep and mysterious. But the words of his mouth flow out of it. The fountains of wisdom we gain from listening well to others will, over time, allow us to gaze into the deep places of their intentions and motivations. The fountains of wisdom we produce from speaking to others will, over time, reveal the deep places of our own. It is always a good idea to test the waters before you speak into a conversation. Sometimes it is better not to say anything at all. Don't just jump in. Test the waters.

PRAYER

Father in Heaven, search the deep places of my heart and expose any lurking monsters there. Change my motivations and my intentions to be clean, pure and full of life that is good. And give me the grace today to discern the motives and intentions of others with heavenly wisdom.

JOURNAL

_____
_____
_____
_____
_____
_____
_____
_____
_____
_____
_____
_____
_____
_____
_____
_____
_____
_____
_____
_____
_____
_____
_____
_____
_____
_____
_____

5. Do the Right Thing

"It is not good to show partiality to the guilty
by perverting the justice due the innocent."
Proverbs 18:5

Casey Anthony. You may remember that name which quickly became the object of public scorn after a Florida jury delivered their not-guilty verdict following a drawn out, heart-wrenching trial in 2008. Casey was charged with the murder of her own two-year old daughter, Caylee Marie. During the trial her defense lawyer, Jose Baez, was cunning and creative, dancing on the emotions of the jurors. He called into question Casey's parents' timing and motives in reporting the child missing, and even suggested that Casey's father may have been the father of the deceased child. The media covered this story from start to finish. The American public had become convinced of Casey's guilt and were hysterical about little Caylee's untimely and undeserved death. When the not-guilty verdict was delivered, millions were outraged. Why were they outraged? Because they believed Casey's guilt was clear and the justice due two-year old Caylee had been perverted. It is human nature for someone to be outraged when they perceive that justice has been perverted.

"Don't judge me." How many times a week do you hear that? "Christians aren't supposed to judge," we think. But is that really true? How is someone to go through life without making judgments about people and the things they do? Jesus's words in Matthew Chapter 7 are often used as a proof-text against judgment: "Do not judge so that you won't be judged," he begins. But as he continues, the Lord clarifies that making judgments about right and wrong are necessary. There are, however, some guidelines. Firstly, judge others how you would like to be judged—"for you will be judged with the same standard with which you judge others." Secondly, judge yourself and cleanse yourself before you judge another—"take the plank out of your own eye and then you will see clearly to take the splinter out of your brother's eye." Judgment God's way becomes a gift to both the judge and the one being judged. It provides a healthy pathway toward cleansing, repentance and forgiveness on all sides.

Judgment God's way also paves the way for justice. You don't go through life without making judgments about what is right and what is wrong. Nor should you. Deuteronomy 16:19 and Habakkuk 1:4 also reveal God's heart toward justice. But justice is a mere fairy tale without judgment. How is justice to be delivered if a judgment about right and wrong is not made? And how is judgment about right and wrong to be made unless someone weighs competing claims in the balance and prayerfully measures them against timeless truth? How is someone to do the right thing unless he makes judgments between what is right and what is wrong?

I am constantly amazed, and frustrated, by the "good-ole-boy" culture. We too often—and too readily—look over evils committed by our friends. Ancient wisdom says this is nothing more than a perversion of justice for the innocent. Wrong is always wrong no matter who commits it. And justice is always just no matter to whom it is due.

Making judgments about right and wrong are easier when we are emotionally and relationally removed from the offense. We can see all sides much more clearly if our social circle is not immediately involved. But when someone we know or love is tangled in a mess of injustice, lines tend to blur and judgments soften. In going social in a socially radioactive culture, we often worry that choosing a side or standing for what is right will sever friendships. So when justice is due on a smaller, more personal scale it is more frequently perverted by those who refuse to judge.

Often, delivering justice is difficult. Especially when the offender is inside our friendship circle, doing the right thing can be costly. Delivering justice often costs us money, time, energy, and even friendships. But every second justice is delayed, the innocent suffer from the corruption of what is upright. Part of going social is making judgments about what is right and what is wrong. Relational connections can sometimes blur those lines. But ancient wisdom clears them up. And the cost is never too great to do the right thing. Part of living in community is owning guilt and repenting from it. Part of living in community is also championing the innocent and delivering justice for the guilty.

The truth is, you and every one of your friends are imperfect people. Every one of us is a real person with real problems. I work within a denominational structure that is currently experiencing the publicized moral failures of an unprecedented number of exalted leaders. Thankfully, to date, there has been no perversion of justice due the innocent victims who have been affected by their wrongdoing. I am thankful that our denomination's constituents and boards are doing the right things. But this season of moral upheaval within the ranks of those whom we have trusted most has turned the stomach of us all. What we are beginning to realize is what I heard Jimmy Draper say one afternoon: every one of us is entirely capable of the worst evils we can possibly imagine. We were created by God, for God, in God's image. But, in the Garden of Eden, the very millisecond humanity desired the knowledge of right and wrong, we chose wrong over right. The natural direction of a sin-stained soul is not toward God but away from him—not toward righteousness, but away from it.

In going social, we should expect that ourselves and every one of our friends at some point will do the wrong thing. In one way or another, we will all eventually (often repeatedly) commit some offense against an innocent other. Ancient wisdom would teach us that if our commitment to our friends is a righteous one, then our commitment to justice is for their benefit. True friends are not yes-men or yes-women who will blindly side with you regardless the circumstances. Rather, true friends are those who have the freedom to correct you when you are wrong, and who will allow you to do the same for them.

Since offense is inherent and common to the fallen human condition, apology and forgiveness must also become a normal part of healthy friendships. When someone in your social circle does the wrong thing, whether it is you who are offended or a third party, it is a gift from God to him or her that you might pull the plank out of your own eye first, then help your friend remove the splinter from his or hers.

Sometimes doing the right thing means owning guilt and repenting from it that you might be restored. Sometimes doing the right thing means helping others see their guilt and paving for them a pathway toward repentance and restoration. In either occasion, every second the right thing is delayed justice is perverted for the innocent. Judge yourself first. Get the plank out of your own eye. Then you will be able to see clearly enough to help your friend remove the speck from his.

Are you quick to compromise justice when the guilty party is a friend or a person of notoriety? Do you sometimes forget that both the guilty and the innocent—no matter who they are—are owed your commitment to unadulterated justice? Going social God's way means that it is always the right time to do the right thing, and always the wrong time to do the wrong thing.

PRAYER

God, according to your great mercy, you have given us ancient wisdom by which to judge right from wrong. You are the just and righteous God of the ages. Teach me to love justice and innocence no matter the parties involved on either side. Make me a good friend who does the right thing and paves pathways for others to do the same.

JOURNAL

_____
_____
_____
_____
_____
_____
_____
_____
_____
_____
_____
_____
_____
_____
_____
_____
_____
_____
_____
_____
_____
_____
_____
_____
_____
_____
_____
_____
_____
_____
_____
_____

6. Measure Your Words

"A fool's lips lead to strife
and his mouth provokes a beating."
Proverbs 18:6

The Washington Post ran an article in 2015 about America's obsession with kissing, entitled, "A Kiss Is Not A Kiss." There is no doubt our culture has romanticized these muscled mouth-flaps through the years for purposes ranging from personal pleasure to sensual advertisement. While you are watching television today, give a close look to the commercials and notice how the lips are highlighted or emphasized to sell just about everything. The Washington Post's article included some rather interesting (disturbing?) research from livescience.com and psychologytoday.com. The bad news is locking lips for 10 seconds allows for the exchange of up to 80 million bacteria. The good news is the same kiss can exercise up to 146 muscles and burn five calories. Even exchange? You decide.

The average American spends over 20,000 minutes of his or her life kissing someone else. Interestingly enough, locking lips is only common to less than half of the world's cultures. Those cultures who do not kiss are disgusted at the thought of locking lips. However you feel about the lips, ancient wisdom gives a clear warning: "A beautiful woman who rejects good sense is like a gold ring in a pig's snout," (Proverbs 11:22).

Contemporary reiterations of this proverb begin something like this: "You can put lipstick on a pig, but it's still a pig."

There is nothing profitably romantic about a fool's lips. Oh, they may drip with sensual pleasure and wet the appetite of those less discerning. But ultimately, nothing wise and nothing beneficial rolls off the lips of a fool. If you thought 80 million bacteria sounded off-putting, consider the ancient wisdom of Proverbs 18:5: "a fool's lips lead to strife and his mouth provokes a beating."

I have the distinct pleasure of knowing quite a few such fools. For some reason they are surprised that their coarse language and controversial conversational content always ends up in a fight. "I can't help it," such a fool protests. "It's just how I am. I speak my mind and if you don't like it, too bad." In other words, "I really don't care how my words make you feel. And if you have a problem with it, let's box." The offended party's outrage gives the foolish communicator some feeling of accomplishment. He welcomes the fight because deep down he believes it justifies his self-proclaimed virtuous position.

Some fools, you will discern, say things for the exact purpose of creating tension and stirring controversy. I have noticed that in my day Twitter is a hotbed for such foolish communication. If you can craft a 280-character statement that insights rage and indignation within the mind of your opponents, you just might get ten-thousand comments and perhaps the same number of retweets. In so doing, you have become a hero among those who share your opinion and a target among those who do not. It amazes me that even Christian pastors, many of whom I love and respect, will engage in such foolish activity. Taking a firm but humble stand on an important issue is one thing. The purposeful stimulation of anger in your reader is something completely different. If the truth angers, so be it. But if the way I present the truth is crafted for the purpose of inducing outrage, foolishness is my only recompense. A foolish person enjoys the fight. A wise person longs for peace.

I sat in a Starbucks one afternoon last week passing time before a scheduled meeting. As I often do, I had brought my Bible and computer in with me with plans to study and write. Soon a man walked in with his Bible in hand. After quickly scanning the room, he made a straight line for me.

He said, "I love to see people in here reading their Bibles. Can you explain it to me?" To which I replied, "Well, maybe you can explain it to me. Have a seat," and I made room to welcome him at my table. He sat across from me and unzipped his Bible case. For forty-five seconds he was cordial. For the following forty-five minutes, he was explosive. He had crafted leading questions to dig out of me my beliefs about certain things in the Bible then, true to his obviously rehearsed bait-and-switch methodology, stuck his finger in my face and called me a false prophet and a false teacher. For forty-five minutes. Out loud. With people watching.

Thankfully, the Lord has gifted me with a disposition that is not easily offended and is rarely angered. So I listened to his arguments as they rolled off his tongue. I answered his arguments from Scripture, when he let me. What stunned me is that we had the same belief about the message and nature of salvation—by grace alone through faith in Jesus Christ alone. His anger toward me was over peripheral issues. He kept getting loud and standing up. I would gently invite him to sit back down and have a conversation. But after forty-five minutes of literally sticking his finger in my face and belligerently accusing me of being a false prophet and a false teacher, we had gained no ground. My heart hurts for this man because he longs for controversy and altercation. Somehow, he honestly believes that if he can get someone as angry or more angry than himself over these particular theological leanings, he has been successful. A fool's lips lead to strife. And his mouth provokes a beating.

In going social, the wise person will measure out his or her words carefully, as always to communicate graciously and peacefully. How are your words measured out? If effective communication is on one side of the scale and belligerent self-justification on the other, how does the scale tip when you speak? Our natural tendency is to prove ourselves right while justifying our emotions against another's reactions. But if your standards of measurement are limited to your own emotions and someone else's reactions, you will have a rollercoaster of a conversational life. Your lips will lead to nothing but conflict, your points will never be proven, you will make more enemies than friends and you will consistently demonstrate yourself a fool. Lipstick on a pig.

When we share our lives with others in meaningful community, disagreement is guaranteed. Sometimes our disagreements are minor and sometimes they are major. Ancient wisdom would tell us that no matter how attractive or experienced a set of lips may be, if they regularly provoke conflict they are nothing more than the flapping gates to a fool's self-righteousness.

So how do you feel about performing a personal conversational inventory today? Sometimes conflict is unavoidable. I get that. But how you respond to what others say is your responsibility. You can choose to fight with the fool. Or you can choose to either diffuse or dismiss a foolish conversation. Remember, if you kiss a pig wearing lipstick you end up wearing the lipstick of a pig. Don't let the 80 million forms of social bacteria from a fool's lips be found in your mouth, too. Measure your words against this ancient wisdom: Am I quick to provoke wrath with my words, or do I value the gentleness and kindness of controversial conversational engagement that are fruits of God's Spirit (Galatians 5:22)?

PRAYER

Spirit of God, at all times help me to measure my words with love and grace. Let me not speak foolishly today, leading to strife or conflict. Keep me from loving self-justification more than effective communication. Fill my mouth with ancient wisdom to speak truth in love in every circumstance.

JOURNAL

_____
_____
_____
_____
_____
_____
_____
_____
_____
_____
_____
_____
_____
_____
_____
_____
_____
_____
_____
_____
_____
_____
_____
_____
_____
_____
_____
_____
_____

7. Lies Imprison, Truth Liberates

"A fool's mouth is his devastation
and his lips are a trap for his life."
Proverbs 18:7

Not only will a fool's mouth lead to strife and a beating (v.6), but it will eventually bring about his own destruction. Vanessa and I used to watch a series on Food Network titled "Dinner Impossible." Celebrity Chef Robert Irvine would go into a restaurant doomed for imminent closure. He would counsel the owner, review and change the menu, invest a few thousand dollars, train the team of chefs and waiters/waitresses and plan a day for reopening. His methods proved extremely successful. The problem, however, was that his resume that got him hired for this job contained a few embellishments of the truth. For example, he claimed to have designed the cake for the royal wedding of Prince Charles and Princess Diana when in fact he was only a student at the school where it was made. Other exaggerations were uncovered on his resume as well leading to his abrupt and rather unceremonious removal. The very lies that got him hired to his own television show in 2007 got him fired from it in 2008. As it turns out, he fell into his own trap of lies. After a period of waiting, Irvine was eventually restored to his television show, but not without an embarrassing public spectacle that undermined his integrity.

Did you teach your children how to lie? I didn't. Somehow, they just learned how to do that all on their own. People generally lie for one of two reasons: either to get out of trouble, or to construct a false positive impression of themselves. Either way, lies are terrible things. It takes much more work to keep up with a lie than it does to be forthcoming with the truth. As Mark Twain once said, "If you tell the truth you don't have to remember anything." Lies build on top of lies and their unstable, shifting sands eventually bring the tower down. It is a lot of work to keep up with a lie and anything you build atop it is doomed for devastation. Better to just tell the truth and build something with structural integrity instead.

Lies are intended to set traps for the listener. With them, the communicator deceives his listener with surreptitious allure, inviting anyone who will believe into the tangled web of his own impending destruction. Lies imprison both those who tell and those who believe. The four surrounding walls are constructed of deception, malice, restlessness and selfish ambition. Only a fool would invite others into his own rotting cell to share in his eventual misery.

The only light in such a dismal, punitive chamber is found in looking upward, to the truth. The fool keeps this heavenward window covered at all costs knowing that once the light is discovered, his secrets will be unveiled. Only when the uncorrupted truth is welcomed into a situation can those entangled see the issue with clarity. There, in the light of the truth, twisted cords will be unraveled and impure motivations exposed. "For nothing is concealed that won't be revealed, and nothing hidden that won't be made known and brought to light," (Luke 8:17). "You will know the truth, and the truth will set you free," (John 8:32). Lies imprison. Truth liberates.

The habitual liar. This fool lies because that's just what he does; it is part of his social DNA. He will lie about his name to strangers, about what he just ate to his friends or about his favorite ice cream flavor to his own family. Lying is the habitual liar's way of sociologically creating his own world by feeding off the gullibility of others. There, in his own little world, the fool is enthroned as the uncontested king. When his lies are exposed he will either cover it with another lie or divert attention by calling out the lies of his opposition. Ultimately he falls into his own trap when no one believes even the least significant of things he claims. His own little world becomes his own little prison cell where he turns out to be the gullible one, convinced of his own destructive sociopathic delusions.

The compulsive liar. Such a fool's default setting is to lie. He does not have the preconceived delusional intentions of the habitual liar, but when he is put on the spot lies roll off his lips before the truth can even be formulated in his mind. Compulsive liars fear not having an answer more than they fear being wrong. The traps they set for their listeners are traps of false wisdom, false humility and false concern. No matter the stimuli, their sociological reflex is to respond with a lie. Like your doctor's little rubber hammer exciting your patellar tendon, the compulsive liar spits untruth thoughtlessly, on the spot. Repeatedly, this fool falls into his own trap by convincing himself that his lies are born from pure motives.

The opportune liar. This fool lurks in the conversational shadows until an opportune moment presents itself. Normally uninvolved in lies or gossip, he will jump on board when it serves his own interests. The opportune liar prefers to join in others' traps of lies instead of creating his own. But as with any other lie, the trap he endorses will eventually swallow him up along with the others who advance it.

The fool does not have the capacity to understand that his lies are just as destructive to himself (if not more destructive to himself) than they are to those who believe them. When a wise person goes social, prisoners are set free. When a fool goes social, people are bound by the recklessness of a lie. A fool is never more foolish than when he fails to see that the reckless snare he has set for someone else will eventually be his own demise. "A fool's mouth is his devastation, and his lips are a trap for his life."

Do you know anyone who might be characterized as a habitual, compulsive or opportune liar? Do you fall into one of those categories yourself? In our day of going social, are you the same person across your multiple social platforms? Or are you intentionally deceiving some on one social platform while trying to maintain a true identity among others on another social platform? Which one is the real you? Perhaps that question deserves more attention than you just afforded it: Which one is the real you?

Do you often promote yourself at the expense of the purity of the truth? Do you set traps with your words, hoping someone will fall in? Do you drag others into your conversational charades? Come clean, or you will soon find yourself a victim of your own demise.

In his iconic Sermon on the Mount, Jesus summed it up as succinctly as I have ever heard or read: "Let your 'yes' mean 'yes' and your 'no' mean 'no,'" (Matthew 5:37). Communication should be a tool for cultivating meaningful relationships not for building our own imaginary kingdoms on foundations of sand. A fool's lies will eventually find him out. Wherever lies lead, devastation, heartache and shame always follow. Telling the truth should be as simple as letting your "yes" mean "yes" and your "no" mean "no." Anything more complicated than that is a trap—one that is set for the hearer, but will eventually bring about the ruin of the teller. Count on it.

PRAYER

God, give me the grace today to speak words that set people free, not words that imprison them. Remove from me the urge to set traps for others and help me respond with grace when they fall into the traps they have set for themselves.

JOURNAL

_____
_____
_____
_____
_____
_____
_____
_____
_____
_____
_____
_____
_____
_____
_____
_____
_____
_____
_____
_____
_____
_____
_____
_____
_____
_____
_____
_____
_____
_____

.

8. Don't Gossip

"A gossip's words are like choice food
that goes down to one's innermost being."
Proverbs 18:8

Vanessa and I tried a new local restaurant on our date night a few weeks ago. It's never a good sign when you walk in at 6pm on a Friday night and you are the only customers. Nevertheless, we decided to give it a shot. As it turns out, the food was unreasonably expensive. That explained the customer vacuum. We do not normally spend that much money on ourselves, but we were already seated and enjoying each others' company.

Appetizers were okay. The service was nothing spectacular. We ordered the "Surf and Turf" as an entrée to share. Vanessa would eat the lobster tail and I would take care of the bacon-wrapped filet mignon. Oh... My... Word... The steak absolutely melted in my mouth, every bite a masterpiece. Seriously, I have never had a steak so delicious. It was amazing. The whole way home it's all I could talk about. The next week I met her at a much more reasonably priced steakhouse where we have eaten together many times. However, my steak there did not bring me much satisfaction. My palate couldn't help but draw the comparisons. If I had my choice, it would be that delectable bacon wrapped filet mignon from the other restaurant every time. If my wallet had its choice, it would be Arby's every time. If my medical doctor had his choice, it would be grilled chicken and salad every time. Turns out even the choicest, most mouth-watering of finely prepared steaks is bad for my cholesterol level. Not all good food is good for you.

What is gossip? Gossip is something told in secret that, whether true or untrue, alters someone else's reputation. The textbook definition from Dictionary.com reads this way: "idle talk or rumor, especially about the personal or private affairs of others." Often gossip is malicious, but it does not have to be. Sometimes gossip is simply the stealing of information-telling privilege—telling information to others that is not your information to tell. Whispering the news of someone's newly discovered pregnancy, for example. Or burning up the phones with a friend's recently discovered health issue after he or she has specifically asked that you tell no one (even if you disguise it as a "prayer request").

Everyone's taste buds are different, but it is human nature that gossip (secret information) entices the pallets of us all. Gossip is delicious, as is all sin. If sin did not promise gratification of some kind, no one would be tempted. Gossip is a charming, deadly woman dressed in pearls and lace. She aims to seduce us all. Knowing something others do not know—having inside information—being in the loop when others are not—these longings expose the depraved tendency of every one of us, to elevate knowledge above wisdom. In essence, that's what gossip is: the elevation of knowledge above wisdom.

Consider the words of this anonymous poem:

My Name Is Gossip. I have no respect for justice. I maim without killing. I break hearts and ruin lives. I am cunning and malicious and gather strength with age.

The more I am quoted the more I am believed. I flourish at every level of society. My victims are helpless. They cannot protect themselves against me because I have no name and no face.

To track me down is impossible. The harder you try, the more elusive I become. I am nobody's friend. Once I tarnish a reputation, it is never the same. I topple governments and ruin marriages. I ruin careers and cause sleepless nights, heartache and indigestion. I spawn suspicion and generate grief.

I make innocent people cry in their pillows. Even my name hisses. I AM CALLED GOSSIP.

It should come at no surprise that the Book of Proverbs—a book of wisdom—includes some form of instruction about the tongue, speech or words in almost every single chapter. The most often quoted of which being, "Life and death are in the power of the tongue," (Proverbs 18:21. We will deal more exhaustively with this verse in Chapter 21). The tongue is either a tool to build or a weapon to destroy. It amazes me that followers of Jesus spend so much of their energy in judgment of other's failures, faults and sins while completely ignoring the relational and spiritual devastation that comes from inappropriate uses of the tongue, gossip being the choice abuse among most believers in closed circles.

Just like I would naturally choose the expensive steak over the less expensive one, we all have the inherent propensity to choose gossip when it is an option on the menu. The appeal of gossip is that it delights the pallet and fills the belly. It promises both immediate gratification and lasting pleasure. When we are in the presence of those ignorant, through gossip we can prove ourselves enlightened. Then when they enlighten others, it is by our illumination they have illuminated. Gossip is a sin that keeps on giving. It both delights the pallet and fills the belly.

But ancient wisdom warns us that not all good food is good for you. Healthy conversations nourish the body, but gossip rots the soul. It clogs the spiritual arteries and produces layers of fat around a calloused heart.

It has been said that knowledge is power. But to quote Uncle Ben's words of timely wisdom to his nephew Peter (Spiderman), "With great power comes great responsibility." A gossip wants all the power of knowing but none of the responsibility that comes along with it. The king's words in Proverbs 18:8 describe the satisfaction of gossip as going down "to one's innermost being." Literally, "the chambers of the belly." Those who get fat on gossip are irresponsible consumers of knowledge. After a while, such a fool fails to even recognize when he is gossiping because a lack of self-control has permitted the taste of this evil to become typical on his tongue. He is incapable of enjoying the delicacies of finer foods such as discernment, grace, trustworthiness and respect.

A number of years ago I was on the phone with an older Christian woman. Within only a few minutes it became obvious to me that the whole reason for her call was to gossip about other people in the church and the community. I stopped her in mid-sentence and said, "I'm sorry, Mrs. Smith but this sounds a whole lot like gossip to me and I really don't want to have anything to do with it. Is there something else you'd like to talk about, or something I can help you with?" She was offended and hung up the phone in embarrassment. I wish I could say it led to immediate repentance and restoration, but she left the church and never spoke to me again.

If you recognize that you are on the receiving end of gossip, immediately redirect the conversation, cut it off or get out of there. Recognize the danger as soon as possible and take action. In the end the benefit to you will be great, and prayerfully, the gossiper may learn repentance in the process. If you find yourself on the delivering end of gossip, remove not just the words from your mouth but the desire for it from your heart. Learn to satisfy your palate and your belly with good food that is good for you. Learn to value wisdom over knowledge. And learn that with whatever knowledge you have, responsibility has come along with it. Why lend your tongue as an instrument unto death, when it can be such a powerful tool unto life? Will you use your tongue as a tool to build, or a weapon to destroy?

PRAYER

Father in Heaven, help me to quickly recognize gossip when it comes my way and give me the self-control to reject its deceitful promise of fulfillment. Teach me to value wisdom over knowledge. Make my innermost being pure and healthy, uncorrupted by the foolishness of gossip.

JOURNAL

_____
_____
_____
_____
_____
_____
_____
_____
_____
_____
_____
_____
_____
_____
_____
_____
_____
_____
_____
_____
_____
_____
_____
_____
_____
_____
_____
_____
_____

9. Eliminate Laziness, Embrace Diligence

"The one who is lazy in his work
is brother to a vandal."
Proverbs 18:9

To my parents, I am the youngest of five sons. That's right, five sons. No girls. And I am their favorite son... wait, I meant youngest. My Dad was and still is a pastor, and I don't think he knows how to spell the word "lazy." In fact, he retired about five years ago and I don't think he knows how to spell the word "retired" either. If the man is not working on something, he is asleep (and he does not do much of that). When we were kids he would wake us up at 7:00 on a Saturday morning and have us in the yard mowing grass or trimming trees before any of our friends even peeled open an eyelid. Anything that needed to be done, we figured out how to do it ourselves—from changing the oil in our vehicles to replacing the roof on our house. Dad modeled a strong work ethic. He instilled this into his sons. And to this day that strong work ethic he instilled within us has proven invaluable for all five of us at work, at home and at play.

Much of the Proverbs is devoted to the rebuke of a lazy man. God is the God of activity—of work: "When God had completed all His work... He rested... from all His work," (Genesis 2:2). Even before The Fall, work was an intrinsic joy for mankind: "God took the man and placed him in the garden of Eden to work it and watch over it," (v.15). Work itself is not a curse. Rather, it is a gift from God. How gracious is this Creator, that he would form mankind in his image and after his likeness—the pinnacle of all his creative endeavor—then extend to us the honor of working with him to cultivate and care for the earth?! How foolish of us to deny the goodness of our cultivating work in favor of self-deprecating slothfulness? Both at work and at home, there is a God-sized and God-shaped difference between rest and slothfulness. Rest comes after work, not before it. The wise man is to be a hard worker both in the field and at home. And he is to enjoy the rest that comes as the cultivation of fulfillment by his own hands.

The opposite of laziness is diligence. Just as God was diligent in His work of creation, man should be diligent in his work of creation cultivation and creation care. At work, the man and woman should be using the creative intelligence with which God has gifted them to make the earth produce good things it otherwise would not have produced. Consider the benefits of diligent work in the field of transportation alone: from walking to rolling to riding to flying. Wow! When coupled with diligence, mankind's intelligence and creativity have almost unlimited potential. When coupled with laziness, that creative initiative is woefully suppressed. Diligence produces innovation and maximized potential. Laziness produces nothing.

Solomon's proverbs have an interesting way of getting a point across. Here, he writes that a lazy person "is brother to a vandal." A "brother" in the text just means a kinfolk of some kind, related or unrelated, whether literal or metaphorical. This is the wise king's way of saying that the one is just like the other. The lazy person is just like the vandal. This point is necessary because most lazy people assume their laziness is not really hurting anything. Ancient wisdom sees it differently. The lazy one is just like the "master of destruction," (this is the literal translation of "vandal" in the verse). Laziness in one's work ethic—lack of commitment and diligence—ultimately lends itself to destruction. The way ancient wisdom sees it, at all times one is either constructing or destructing.

I have had the privilege of destroying a few houses. I say "privilege" because there honestly is something cathartic about taking a sledgehammer to something, especially after a long day. Houses that are beyond repair are sometimes best torn down. Have you ever stepped foot in a house that has not been lived in for a while? You would think that a structure uncorrupted by daily interaction with a human being should remain unspoiled by what humans bring into it. However, without someone there to wipe the baseboards, clean the floor, adjust the screws/nails, dust the cabinets, repair the roof from the elements' damage, and apply the daily pressure of just walking on the floors, a house dilapidates rather quickly. Without regular human activity—work—the structure is not only useless in its purpose, but is eventually destroyed. In the perspective of the wise king, the outright destroyer is no worse than the lazy worker and the lazy worker is no better than the outright destroyer. They are brothers. They are one and the same.

What are you destroying through your inactivity? Laziness destroys much more than housing structures. Laziness destroys marriages, families, work relationships, churches, communities, partnerships and much more. Anything that is worth having is worth working for, both to gain and to maintain.

There is an old Korean folktale about a lazy boy named Bae. Bae despised work so much that he just wanted to sleep all day, every day. He longed to be a cow because cows, he thought, just rested and ate grass all day. He ran away from home and met a merchant in the village who pretended to sympathize with his plight. The merchant magically turned the boy into a cow and sold him to a farmer. To Bae's surprise, the farmer actually expected the cow to work by pulling a plow and carrying a load. The cow longed to be his former self, where he could enjoy his family and friends again. His longing became reality and he was restored to his family and friends, never to despise work again.

Going social is not for lazy cows. Going social takes work. It takes work to keep up with the relationships that matter in your life, and to serve them. Additionally, how you physically labor at work and at home builds the foundation for social interaction. Laziness at work lends itself to strained relationships among coworkers. Laziness at home lends itself to strained relationships among family. Laziness at play lends itself to strained relationships with friends. And as the proverb says, laziness is brother to destruction. God designed humankind to be diligent in every sphere of social life. When we are diligent, we build and cultivate. When we are not diligent, we destroy.

Are you lazy at work? At home? Among friends? Is your laziness driving a wedge between you and others? The trick is to learn to value the relationship more than you value the idleness. Work cultivates, builds and creates. Laziness corrupts, extinguishes and destroys. Everything in your life that is worth having is worth working for—both to gain and to maintain. "The one who is lazy in his work is brother to a vandal." The one who idly allows things to fall apart is no different from the one who actively tears them down. Whether pertaining to the cultivation and care of creation or the cultivation and care of relationships, either work with diligence to build it up or whatever it is will slowly be torn down.

PRAYER

In all of the work you have called me to today, Lord, you have called me to excellence and diligence in it. Give me the endurance and the self-control to work with diligence today—to be a builder, not a destroyer, of good things.

JOURNAL

_____
_____
_____
_____
_____
_____
_____
_____
_____
_____
_____
_____
_____
_____
_____
_____
_____
_____
_____
_____
_____
_____
_____
_____
_____
_____
_____
_____

GOING SOCIAL

10. Run to the Lord

"The name of the Lord is a strong tower;
the righteous run to it and are protected."
Proverbs 18:10

Do you know what a fail-safe is? It's something embedded within a particular system or structure that is designed to ensure safety when failure occurs. Fail-safes do not prevent the failure of systems or structures. Rather, they are designed with rescue in mind. They exist to make a bad situation better than it could have been. Traffic lights, for example, are programmed with a fail-safe code to blink red on all sides in the event the main control board goes down. Most elevators have a fail-safe break system installed that automatically engages if a cable snaps. Buildings where large numbers of people gather at a time (such as schools, shopping malls, some church buildings, etc.) are usually equipped with a fail-safe generator which kicks in only seconds after a main power outage.

What about in an awkward or potentially dangerous social failure—what fail-safe do you have? Some have the habit of talking too much when they sense social failure. The mouth starts moving and words are coming out; they are saying a lot of things without really saying anything at all. Others resort to inopportune sarcasm when they sense impending social failure. Sarcasm is not bad in itself, but when it is an ill-timed or inappropriate tactic to salvage your relational mojo, it's not a good idea. Perhaps you have run across someone whose social fail-safe is diversion. By saying something positive or negative about someone else, they hope to divert attention away from the topic at hand. Others use a headache or stomach problems as their fail-safe. If the conversation is not going how they would like, the trusty old fall back is, "I don't feel so good." Some employ much more serious measures as fail-safes: drugs, alcohol, violence, sex. Social fail-safes are what you run to when you feel like things are going or have gone bad. So how about it? What's your social fail-safe?

The second half of this proverb refers to "the righteous" as a group of people. Living righteously (right-doing) is like living in a warzone, no matter the generation or culture. Going social in a world irreparably scarred by sin and full of sinful people, if you do the wrong things you will be praised, encouraged and even called a hero. But if you do the right things, you will often be ridiculed, hated and fought against vigorously. What else is a righteous person to expect going social in a world that is characterized by blatant unrighteousness?

But there is a refuge—a strong tower—for the righteous one who is desperate for safe harbor in the middle of life's war. Protection, safety, and strength are found when the righteous person runs to "the name of the Lord." His name is Yahweh, the great I AM. Jesus Christ, the Alpha and Omega. He is the Lord of heaven and earth. With a simple word he spoke the universe into existence (Genesis 1). By this same powerful word he currently sustains the universe's existence (Hebrews 1:3). One day in the future the word of his mouth will judge the nations in righteousness (Revelation 19:15). When the righteous take refuge in the name of the Lord, they are protected. They are safe from the enemy and from all those who wield his weapons of warfare.

The name of the Lord is much more than a fail-safe for social experiments gone wrong. The name of the Lord is a fortress of protection at all times for those who find themselves in his righteousness. If you are running to, walking to, limping to or crawling to the name of the Lord for refuge, know that righteousness is the price of admission. Ultimately, none of us is righteous—"not even one," (Romans 3:10-12). But the Bible says, in Romans 5:1, that the Lord Jesus Christ is our righteousness. Run to the name of Jesus and the fortress of God's protection is something that never leaves you. Wherever he goes and whatever battle he is fighting, the righteous one who has run to the name of Jesus is safe—protected—from the enemy. When you are safely harbored in the fortress of God's strong name, "The Lord will fight for you. You need only be still," (Exodus 14:14).

In my mid and late twenties I enjoyed watching UFC matches. I followed certain fighters and watched every fight. A few friends would often join me at a local buffalo wings place to watch title matches on the big screen. As my firstborn son began to grow and mature, we would rumble on the floor a bit. I'd put him in a rear naked choke hold or pretend to lock him up in an arm bar. It was all in good fun. Until it wasn't. I was a worship pastor at the time and my youth pastor's family was over at the house. His son was the same age as mine. The two of them were in the living room hanging out together while the rest of us were in the kitchen. "Daaaaaad!!!" … "Daaaaaad!!!" It wasn't my son's voice. But we both ran into the living room to see that my son had his son in a perfect arm bar and was fully committed, saying, "Tap out! Tap out!" Instead, all that came out of his little friend's mouth was, "Daaaaaad!!!"

In the moment, I confess I didn't know whether to be proud or concerned. Both dads rushed in to help. Our guests' return trip home was expedited that night and conversations for the next several weeks were a bit awkward. But this little boy had learned something in that moment I hope he never forgot as he grew. He could have gotten out of that situation a number of different ways. But he knew the best thing to do was to call out to his dad. Even if everything else failed him, his dad would not. His dad was a strong tower. A refuge in all kinds of trouble.

Do you know whose name to call when you're in trouble? When going social feels like interpersonal warfare, remember that there is no fail-safe mechanism you can employ that will rescue you like the name of Jesus can. When you are embarrassed, let Jesus be your hiding place. Find yourself secure there in his strong arms, regardless of what anyone else would say. When you are angered, let Jesus be your cool-down chamber. Find the self-control you need there in the cool breeze of his fellowship, owning your emotions and choosing to respond in grace. When you are confused, let Jesus be your think-tank. Immerse yourself in his Word to find wisdom and clarity for the moment. Whatever danger you face in going social today, ancient wisdom would say, "run to Jesus." There alone will you find strength and protection in your time of need.

Ultimately, when danger is on the horizon in our social lives all of our subconscious fail-safes are designed either to save our reputations or to make us feel better about ourselves. Like concave and convex mirrors in a silly maze at the county fair, these social fail-safes distort reality to make us feel things and think things that are simply not true. The psychological games we attempt to impose on others end up putting us in checkmate, ourselves.

I have great news for you, though. If the name of Jesus is where you run, the mirrors inside that strong tower always reflect an accurate image of who you are. Inside the name of the Lord you will always see yourself as someone created in the image of God—beautiful by design and designed for a beautiful purpose. In the name of Jesus every stain is cleaned, every spot is covered and every scar is perfected. In the name of Jesus there is no part of you that is left unprotected. There is no shame there. No fear. No worry. No hate. No regret. Just you, exactly how God sees you: loved, chosen, redeemed. When going social goes bad, run to Jesus. Run to the Lord.

PRAYER

Oh Lord, in the heat of every battle today, hide me in the strong tower of your great name. Thank you for salvation in the name of Jesus. Keep me safe from evil there. Protect me. When going social goes sour and my first instinct is to run to anything else, remind me to instead take refuge in the name of the Lord.

JOURNAL

_____
_____
_____
_____
_____
_____
_____
_____
_____
_____
_____
_____
_____
_____
_____
_____
_____
_____
_____
_____
_____
_____
_____
_____
_____
_____
_____
_____
_____

11. Money Is Not the Answer

"The wealth of the rich is his fortified city;
in his imagination it is like a high wall."
Proverbs 18:11

A long time ago in a galaxy not so far away, there was a little boy named Franklin, whose mother taught him how to dip candy in melted chocolate (God bless moms). By the time Franklin was 19 years old he was making, dipping and selling chocolate candies in his hometown in Minnesota. He soon was married and moved to Tacoma, Washington to start a chocolate candy making and dipping business, but he couldn't keep up with the competition and his business failed miserably. He moved his family back home to Minnesota and tried again. There, Franklin Mars founded the Mars company and built a factory to mass produce chocolate dipped milkshake-bars he called "Milky Ways." In 1929 Franklin moved the factory to California and subsequently produced the Snickers Bar and the Mars Bar. Can I get an amen?

When Franklin died he passed on the business to his son, Frank Jr. In the mid-1900's the company came up with the craziest idea—to produce colorful, button-shaped chocolates. Can you guess what they called them? That's right: M&M's. Today, Mars Company is the sixth largest privately-owned business in the United States, with over $33 Billion of sales annually.

Upon their father's death in 1999, the three living Mars children— Jacqueline, Forrest Jr. and John—received an inheritance from their father. The Mars children inherited a net worth of almost $27 Billion each! They did nothing to earn this wealth. It was lavished upon them on the basis of their relationship to Franklin Mars Sr., founder of the company, through the graces of his son Forrest.

Now, I know what you're thinking: "God, why didn't you make my dad filthy rich?" But the truth of the matter is, if you are in Christ Jesus your Heavenly Father has lavished on you all of the riches of heaven through the graces of his Son. "Blessed is the God and Father of our Lord Jesus Christ," wrote the Apostle Paul, "who has blessed us with every spiritual blessing in the heavens in Christ," (Ephesians 1:3). If you are a Christian, even when your bank account is in the red you still operate under the incalculable wealth of God's kingdom. When you look at your spiritual bank statement you should see numbers in your account you don't even know how to pronounce. Every spiritual blessing in the heavens is yours. You've got it all, in Christ Jesus.

Did you notice a contrast between Proverbs 18:10 and Proverbs 18:11? The ancient, wise king is disclosing a distinct and immediate contradiction between the strong tower of the Lord's name and the false security that comes from trusting in temporal wealth.

God desires for his riches to flow through the conduits of kingdom giving—through the graces of the man's and woman's wise management. God gives wealth not for temporal pleasure, but for eternal investment. Most of us believe a little more money would solve our problems. But when our hope is in the imaginary high walls of our padded bank accounts we don't run to the name of the Lord and we are not protected from the enemy. It's not that wealth and righteousness are mutually exclusive, but rather that they do not provide the same level of security. Many who are rich with the wealth of this world assume that they do not need God. They have erected a high, green paper wall around their insecurities. But that wall cannot stand, nor can it satisfy the deepest longings of mankind. Let the poor man run to the name of the Lord to find strength and security. Let the rich man also run to the name of the Lord to find strength and security.

As I write this chapter, two more rich and famous Americans have taken their own lives in the past two days—Kate Spade and Anthony

Bourdain. The news media laments their troubled plights and elaborates on the darkness of depression as a mental illness. And surely, it is. Ultimately, though, we are talking about two people who possessed more social connection and more material gain than any of us with our noses in this book will ever know. All the wealth and fame in the world could not protect them from the war of insecurity that was raging in their spirits. Nor could it satisfy their deep longing for significance and hope. Wealth is not bad in itself, but the walls it erects are imaginary and paper-thin. The only real, lasting protection for the rich and for the poor alike—the only refuge, hope, security—is in the name of the Lord Jesus.

In case you haven't noticed, fortified walls keep people safe within by keeping something else out. In the fortress of the Lord's name, evil is kept out while the righteous refugee is safely sheltered inside. However, inside the false, paper-thin walls of wealth it is not evil that is kept out but usually other people. Evil is at home within the imaginary walls of wealth's towers: "For the love of money is a root of all kinds of evil, and by craving it, some have wandered away from the faith and pierced themselves with many pains," (1 Timothy 6:10). Imaginary green, paper-thin walls of wealth do not keep evil out. But they often keep other people out. One who takes refuge in wealth often isolates himself from others around him who can help, if they are only allowed in. When someone chooses friends and builds cliques based on his or her annual salary, the joys of true community are forfeited. One isolated inside such an imaginary fortress cannot see that joy and happiness are as readily available without wealth as they are with it.

Allow me to reiterate that possessing wealth is not bad or unrighteous in itself. I read somewhere recently that if you make an annual salary of at least $32,000 you are in the top 1% of the whole world. When all is considered, most of us are wealthy beyond what we appreciate even by the world's standards. Having wealth is not bad in itself. It's what we do with that wealth and how we allow it to affect us that makes the difference.

When Vanessa and I got married, I was a music minister at a small Baptist church South Louisiana. My annual salary there was $9,000 before taxes. Both of us were going to college full-time and we thought we were doing good when we had enough quarters to go bowl a couple of games on the weekend. I was also teaching clinics and private lessons (I played low brass) all over the New Orleans area, but the money I made from those gigs was barely enough to pay my gas bill back and forth. For a few months Vanessa supplemented our income by working at JC Penny, but that changed not long into her pregnancy with our first son. Times were hard. But they were so good. We had a church family that loved us deeply and friendships that were forged in the fires of simplicity and genuineness.

It was there that God taught us a lesson about money: money is an important thing, but it is certainly not everything. During those years we learned to trust in the Lord and to give back to him faithfully and sacrificially, even when we gave out of poverty. Over the years, our annual intake increased a little bit at a time. But we would learn that if money was the goal, a little more is never enough. No matter what the problem is, money is not the answer.

Going social is not about amassing friends to yourself who fit your lifestyle. If you can't enjoy the simplicity and genuineness of relationships built around something besides monetary wealth, you are missing out on the invaluable depth of authentic friendships. Having monetary wealth is not a bad thing. But if you are not careful those dollar bills will build high, paper-thin walls around your ego. And instead of being a fortress, those walls will quickly become a prison. Don't flaunt your wealth. Don't isolate yourself from others who do not share it. Just be a real person who loves real people. And watch how this ancient wisdom will give you new life in your contemporary relationships.

PRAYER

Father in heaven, thank you for the riches of your grace that are lavished on me in Christ Jesus. Sheltered in your strong name, keep me from the imaginary security of monetary wealth. Show me the joys of genuine friendships with people of all socioeconomic statuses. And remind me to always find my significance and security in you alone.

JOURNAL

_____

_____

_____

_____

_____

_____

_____

_____

_____

_____

_____

_____

_____

_____

_____

_____

_____

_____

_____

_____

_____

_____

_____

_____

_____

12. Just Say No to Pride

"Before his downfall a person's heart is proud,
but humility comes before honor."
Proverbs 18:12

"Just say no." I was an eight year old boy sitting crisscross-applesauce on the carpeted floor of our school's auditorium when I first heard that phrase. Our state's Department of Education had just launched a new strategy to deter kids from getting involved with illegal drugs. McGruff the Crime Dog came to our school assembly and spoke for about 45 minutes on the dangers of drug use and addiction. He warned us of peer pressure, through which kids who are normally uninvolved with such things are drug into (pun intended) something they really don't want to do. McGruff warned us of the bandwagon approach, through which bad kids would seduce good ones into using because, after all, "everybody's doing it." He taught us about uppers, downers, and all-arounders. And we ended the assembly with a hyped-up call and response: "Just say no!" "Just say no!" Louder! "Just say no!" "Just say no!"

Sadly, many of the boys and girls who sat on the carpeted auditorium floor with me that day, reciting the motto loudly with conviction, would fall into the destructive traps of drug usage only a few years later. Just saying no on the carpeted floor of a school building in third grade was easy. But just saying no when actually pressured by their peers and excluded from the bandwagon required a whole different level of self-control. As the decades pass, the battle between self-control and just saying no intensifies. We learn that as dangerous as illegal drugs are to the human experience, there are other pressures in life that are equally as treacherous. Among them is the appeal of pride. Pride is a godless depravity that literally turns the face of God against a man or woman. "God resists the proud but gives grace to the humble," (Proverbs 3:34, James 4:6).

Pride is a toxic drug, genuine humility its only medicament. Honor is not genuine honor if you give it to yourself. When man instigates his own honor, he becomes a consumer of his own pride. Pride brings a fall. Humility brings honor. Consider these excerpts from other places in the Bible:

- "He mocks those who mock, but gives grace to the humble," (Proverbs 3:34).
- "Clothe yourself with humility… Humble yourselves, therefore, under the mighty hand of God, so that he may exalt you in the proper time, casting all your cares on him, because he cares about you," (1 Peter 5:5-6).
- "The pride of mankind will be humbled, and human loftiness will be brought low; the Lord alone will be exalted on that day. For a day is coming against all that is proud and lofty, against all that is lifted up—it will be humbled," (Isaiah 2:11-12).

The Book of Obadiah, only one chapter with 21 short verses, illustrates perfectly that dangers of pride. Sadly, those who are sinfully prideful are most often even prideful about their pride. But every high thing will one day be brought low. Obadiah's prophetic word is a warning to the nation of Edom, who did horrible things to the people of Judah as the Babylonians conquered their kingdom. The Edomites mocked and spit on Judean captives while the Babylonians led them out of their hometown. They scavenged the freshly evicted neighborhoods and stole all the plunder they could carry. They captured runaways and turned them back in to the

Babylonian authorities. Why? Because they could. They were the Edomites—the people who lived in the clefts of the rock. They thought they were untouchable. They thought themselves above everyone else. And it brought them sick, twisted pleasure to rejoice in the downfall of others. Through Obadiah's prophecy, God exposed the pearls of their pride. With all of their self-made glory, their days safely nestled in the clefts of the rock were numbered. "Even from there," said Almighty God, "I will bring you down," (v.4). Consider the pearls of Edom's pride:

- A Presumptuous Heart (vs.1-4)
  - False Security (v.3)
  - False Prosperity (v.4)
- An Inflated Self-Image (vs.5-9)
  - False Glamour (vs.5-6)
  - False Friendships (v.7)
  - False Wisdom (vs.8-9)
- An Offensive Personality (vs.10-14)
  - Offensive in Speech (v.12)
  - Offensive in Exploitation (v.13)
  - Offensive in Cruelty (v.14)
- A Coming Judgment (vs.15-21)
  - Under the Wrath of God (vs.15-16)
  - On the Wrong Side of Redemptive History (vs.17-18)
  - Excluded from the Kingdom of God (vs.19-21)

These pearls of pride belong not just to the Edomites in the 6th Century BC. They are donned by every person throughout history who fails to "Just Say No" to sinful pride. Pride promises big things, but what it delivers is nothing special: a presumptuous heart, an inflated self-image, an offensive personality, and a coming judgment. However, like the Edomites, those who believe they have risen above God's judgment, nestled in the clefts of the rock, cannot perceive their own impending doom. Eventually, Edom was conquered and their people dispelled from their land by the Babylonians—the same Babylonians whom they had praised for conquering and dispelled Judah.

"Before his downfall, a person's heart is proud." God is no respecter of persons. The ancient wisdom that comes from his heart and his hand is not only for a select few, it's for everyone. There are none so lofty they are above God's judgment. There are none so lowly they are below God's grace.

God longs to honor man. Created in his image and after his likeness, God wants to lift up a man whose heart is pure, not proud. But God cannot and will not exalt a prideful man, lest the man think his exaltation is of his own doing. When God allows a man to exalt himself in his pride, how sad a state of affairs is his; under the false blessing of his own hand, his eyes cannot see that he is under the curse of God's hand. The higher a man climbs on his ladder of self-exaltation, the farther he has to fall toward humility. But the one who stays low—the one who speaks, acts and thinks with a heart of humility—he will receive honor from God. And when all is considered, God's honor is eternal while man's praise is fleeting.

I promise that today you will have the opportunity to either think high or think low. Every day we are tempted by the pearls of pride, but we are challenged by God to instead put on the rags of humility. There, in one's humility, grace for the moment is found. But in one's pride, there is only a presumptuous heart, an inflated self-image, an offensive personality and a coming judgment. Even when the pressure is on among your peers, and even though everyone else is doing it, just say no to pride. You will thank yourself later.

PRAYER

Lord, pump my stomach clean from the drug of pride. Teach me to long for the kind of honor that only comes from your hand. Whenever my heart is high, please bring it down gently. Keep me low so that in your time and in your way you can exalt and honor me as you see fit.

JOURNAL

_____

_____

_____

_____

_____

_____

_____

_____

_____

_____

_____

_____

_____

_____

_____

_____

_____

_____

_____

_____

_____

_____

_____

13. Give Them Your Full Attention

"The one who gives an answer before he listens—
this is foolishness and a disgrace for him."
Proverbs 18:13

Social media is great, except when it's not. There are many benefits to online social platforms and there are also many dangers. One such danger—an interesting side-effect of social media—is that it draws out the naturally judgmental inclination of a depraved mind. We make judgments quickly about what others post and we post things ourselves that boast judgments about others. The key is to communicate your point both effectively and succinctly. No one wants to read three paragraphs of content on a Facebook post. Twitter nipped it in the bud by limiting characters per tweet. But most social media users are not competent in this discipline.

Everything we write is written to the exclusion of something else. When we choose which words to write, we are also choosing which words not to write. So when we post content or claim on a complicated, politically charged or potentially divisive topic, what we write is important, what we don't write is important and how/when we write or don't write what we write or don't write is also important.

Add to this the phenomenon of "sharing" something on your social media accounts. In 2016 a research project was undertaken and subsequently covered by the Washington Post that exposed something rather unsettling about the average social media user. Seventy percent of Facebook users will comment on a shared story without even reading the article or watching the video. Sixty percent, across social media platforms, will share content on their own pages without ever actually clicking the link themselves. The headline/title is enough, we think, to formulate an accurate opinion on a given issue. We speak into the conversation without actually listening to the conversation. And we wonder why we can't get along.

Oh how easy it is to formulate opinions and stake claims before we have all of the information, especially in a 280-character Twittosphere where we can all hide behind the security of our keyboards and phone screens. Every person has a story. And until you know their story, you don't know where they're coming from. And if you don't know where they're coming from, you won't understand where they are or where they're going.

Within the past decade I have been shocked to learn that as far as we have come against institutionalized racism in the United States of America, we still have a long way to go. A friend of mine, Dr. Terry Turner, recently released a book entitled *God's Amazing Grace: Reconciling Four Centuries of African American Marriages and Families*. In his book, he traces historical data to build a facts-based, experientially driven foundation for the history of racism in America. As I read through its pages, I found myself learning information I had never heard and beginning to empathize with feelings and thoughts of African Americans I had never considered. Until I sat down to listen, giving their voice my full attention, my opinions and presumptions were ill-informed and naïve. Ancient wisdom would say that speaking into the conversation of racism in America before listening is an exercise in foolishness and utter disgrace.

What conversations are you speaking into without actually listening? People hold strong opinions for a reason. Unless you give them your full attention, you will never know those reasons and you will never understand their opinions. In conversations, especially the ones that are heated for one reason or another, am I listening when the other person is talking or am I silently formulating my rebuttal? Foolish. Disgraceful. The goal in a conversation should never be to show off my opinion (see Chapter 2) or to win an argument. The goal is to understand, and to be understood.

In one of my Masters level pastoral counseling classes the professor introduced us to a book by James Peterson entitled, *Why Don't We Listen Better: Connecting and Communicating in Relationships*. It is well worth the read. In the book, Peterson promoted his "Talker/Listener Card," and gave a printout for its practical usage. During the course, I confess that my thoughts were rather skeptical toward it. But in my own counseling practice over the period of about ten years, I used this card more times than I can remember. The card folds to sit on a tabletop and is labeled "Talker" on one side and "Listener" on the other so that each party is looking at his or her specific role in the conversation while working through a particular conflict. Words are listed under each designation that further explain the role. Basically, when you are the talker you are attempting to communicate your thoughts non-judgmentally, with grace. When you are the listener, you are actively trying to understand the other person's words and feelings. If either side of an argument is formulating a rebuttal while the other person is speaking, the conversation will not be productive. Rather, foolishness and disgrace are all that could be hoped for in such a situation.

Similarly, a sure mark of a fool is to speak into a conversation authoritatively where he has no authority, or informatively where he has no information. When we talk before we listen, we speak into a conversation we do not really understand. You are not doing anyone any favors by speaking from a false position of authority or information. Rather, you are only proving yourself a fool.

Here are some words of advice: when conflict comes, allow the person who is most greatly offended to speak first. It is in the nature of offense that until we feel heard we will not hear. While one is speaking, the other must be actively listening. Listen not only for words, but also for emotions, implications and even for what is *not* being said. The goal is not to prove your point or to catch the other party in a twist of words. The words coming out of their mouths are coming for the sole purpose of communicating ideas and feelings. Don't get so hung up on the words that you miss the ideas and feelings. These ideas and feelings will not be communicated only in the words that roll off the tongue but also in body language, tone and inflection of voice, facial expressions and more. Additionally, communication of ideas and feelings will be either enhanced or disparaged by the history between the two parties and how each feels at the moment. Listening takes work. But if going social is to be productive and meaningful, it is worth the work. Ancient wisdom says that it is both foolish and disgraceful to speak into a conversation when one has not done the diligence to listen.

What conversations are you speaking into in person and on social media? Have you done the diligence to listen and understand those on the opposing side? Are you pursuing a win or are you pursuing a relationship? Do you need to apologize for your foolishness before you can hope to re-enter the conversation in a meaningful way? Don't be foolish. Don't act disgracefully. Listen before you speak.

PRAYER

God, in my fast-paced world, give me the patience to slow down and listen. Give me the humility and the empathy to desire understanding over winning an argument. Remind me that communication is more than talking and hearing. Make me more like Jesus, who himself did not presume, but asked and listened (Mark 10:51).

JOURNAL

_____

_____

_____

_____

_____

_____

_____

_____

_____

_____

_____

_____

_____

_____

_____

_____

_____

_____

_____

_____

_____

_____

_____

_____

_____

_____

14. Stay Positive

"A person's spirit can endure sickness,
but who can survive a broken spirit?"
Proverbs 18:14

Hypochondriasis. From its Greek origin it literally translates, "under the sternal cartilage." It refers to a feeling in the chest cavity that incites an unsearchable sense of discomfort and unease. More recently the word has come to be the designation for a certain mental disorder in which someone is inconsolably fearful that he or she may have one or more undiagnosed and untreated illnesses. The most recent edition of the Diagnostics and Statistics Manual (DSM-5) renames the disease, "illness anxiety disorder,"— a form of a "broken spirit," as ancient wisdom would designate it. A hypochondriac lives every moment of the day under the crippling fear that his or her body is plagued by a physical illness that doctors have not been able to diagnose, thus, has remained untreated. The hypochondriac is unconvinced by medial tests, blood work or psychological counseling. There is no consolation, no relief and no solution.

Many who suffer from this mental illness are completely incapacitated by it. Some work themselves into such an anxious fit that they actually begin to suffer from physical side effects of an incurable mental illness. Stressed and anxious, the adrenal glands pump cortisol quickly throughout the body. High levels of cortisol constantly raging through the physical body increase blood pressure, reduce sleep, produce awful headaches and even negatively affect the stomach and intestines. As it turns out, physical illness is much easier to treat.

Physical sickness is guaranteed in a world that is fallen from perfection and irreparably scarred by the effects of sin. Sicknesses of the body can cause great pain and ultimately will claim a life. But true life is the life within, for those redeemed through repentance from sin and faith in Jesus Christ (1 Timothy 6:19). Temporal life lasts only for a moment, but eternal life has no expiration date. Thus, true health is a healthy spirit and a healthy soul. Physical sickness cannot itself kill the spirit. But if the spirit is sick, the affliction is terminal.

Doctors and psychologists agree that a hypochondriac's mind directly affects his body. A sick spirit will inevitably produce a sick body. A broken spirit will eventually produce a broken body. Notice in the Psalms where wise, ancient lyricists address the need for a healthy spirit over the need for a healthy body: "My flesh and my heart may fail but God is the strength of my heart," and, "Renew a right spirit within me," (Psalms 73:26, 51:10). The spirit will endure through a man's physical sickness if it is secure in the strength of the Lord. Sickness of the body cannot squash or harm the redeemed spirit in any way. But "who can survive a broken spirit?"

Stay positive. Not in a naïve, irresponsibly optimistic way. But rather, stay positive in the strength of a healthy spirit. When you step out of the comfort of your own home, if you are looking for reasons to feel sick you will find them lurking around every corner. The fallen world can be a brutal place. The fool will allow the fear of every potential illness to cripple him from participating beneficially in communal life. He will see community as a threat instead of as a blessing. This does not give license to thoughtless engagement in dangerous activity. Rather, it allows the mind to remind the spirit that generally speaking, things are probably not as bad as they may seem. A sure mark of anxiety is to live as if one's worst fears have already become reality. A sure mark of faith is to trust that the Lord will work all things together for good, for those who love him and are called according to his purposes (Romans 8:28).

A friend from my past comes to mind. Let's call her Shirley. I was the worship leader at a church in Texas, where Shirley had been an active member for over two and a half decades. For many years she had been afflicted with the disease of multiple sclerosis. She took regular treatments and endured much physical therapy. It helped sometimes, and sometimes it didn't. This disease, for Shirley, most greatly affected the facial muscles. It literally hurt her to smile. But I do not recall ever seeing Shirley without one on her face—a smile, that is. She loved to sing in worship services. She was an active worshipper, engaged with her whole body. My memories of her are so sweet, as I looked her direction from the platform. She would have her hands lifted, her face looking upward, smiling, while singing at the top of her lungs. Tears would be streaming down her face. But not because of her emotional connection to the song—rather, because it physically hurt her to worship the way she did. And yet every Sunday morning and every other chance she got, she raised her arms, put a smile on her face, and sang through the pain and through the tears. Multiple sclerosis ravaged her physical body, but it had absolutely no effect on her spirit.

As a Christian counselor I have witnessed the reverse as well. Those with no physical ailment whatsoever are often tormented, sometimes completely debilitated, by their crushed spirits. Even if a broken body is not healed the spirit can still prosper. But if the broken spirit is not mended, no patient can survive.

This is not an appeal toward the power of positive thinking. You can think yourself physically well all you'd like, but if you are not actually well your denial of reality will not make you so. Rather, this ancient wisdom is an appeal toward the power of a redeemed, healthy spirit. The broken body has no effect over a healthy spirit. But a healthy spirit will always endure a broken body.

Do you know anyone like this in your social circles? Do you know a Shirley? Someone who is so secure in his or her relationship with God that they can always see a positive side in any situation? Not childishly or nonsensically. But rather, he or she has the refreshing ability to peer confidently through the pain of today into the hope of tomorrow. They stay positive through the most negative of circumstances. These are the kinds of people who make going social a blessing. They are the kind of people I want to be around. Their healthy spirits have the unique ability to lift the atmosphere of any potentially negative situation into a positive, faith-filled expectation of a more glorious reality.

Ancient wisdom allows the spirit to stay positive in every circumstance. "A person's spirit can endure sickness, but who can survive a broken spirit?" Stay positive in your relationships. Even when things are physically sick, they can still be spiritually healthy. Conflict gives way to opportunity. Arguments carry the potential of deeper understanding. Sorrow paves the way for consolation. Heartache opens the door to overwhelming joy. Stay positive, and watch this ancient wisdom come to life in your contemporary world.

PRAYER

Father, help me at all times to see myself through your eyes. When my body fails, strengthen my spirit in Christ. In my prayers for others, let me recall the importance of interceding for the spirit more than the body. In all circumstances, help me keep my eyes on the joy of eternal life as I endure the heartaches of physical life.

JOURNAL

_____
_____
_____
_____
_____
_____
_____
_____
_____
_____
_____
_____
_____
_____
_____
_____
_____
_____
_____
_____
_____
_____
_____
_____
_____

15. Be Both Knowledgeable and Wise

"The mind of the discerning acquires knowledge,
and the ear of the wise seeks it."
Proverbs 18:15

Look up. Yes, right now. Look up at the ceiling (or whatever structure may be above your head). Let's pretend you have noticed a few irregularities in the beams or the sheetrock above your head. With a quick glance, you have come to see a few small cracks but don't think much about it. Now look up again, and keep looking. Upon a closer look, you have noticed that the cracks are growing. As you stare, the structure above your head is getting closer and closer to your head. It's falling. Right now.

At this point you have two options. You can continue to stare at the falling structure wondering what could have caused the problem. Perhaps you would think through strong winds and thunderstorms over the past week that may have done some damage. Perhaps you have an intelligent, engineering mind and you would think through the physics and logistics of the rate of fall. Perhaps you would think through how to fix it, when you are ready. That's option one. Option two is... get out of the way! For heaven's sake, the roof is going to fall on your head! In a hypothetical situation like this every reasonable person, whether simple minded or intelligent, would see the first option as a foolish one. The second option is the wise one. But when we do not have the luxury of outside (or hypothetical) perspective, the lines between knowledge and wisdom, foolishness and ignorance, are easily blurred.

Our contemporary Western culture often fails to see the difference between knowledge and wisdom. But ancient cultures knew the difference very well. Knowledge is the acquisition and retaining of true information. Wisdom is appropriate action based on the knowledge one has acquired and retained. Knowledge is what one learns. Wisdom is what one does with what is learned. Knowledge is something you gain. Wisdom is something you do. One can be knowledgeable without being wise—for it is possible to possess true knowledge without acting on it wisely. But one cannot be wise without knowledge—for it is impossible to act wisely on information one do not possess.

True to poetic parallelism, the proverb seems to repeat the same truth, only using different words. The temptation is to take the two phrases as synonymous. But although the form is poetic parallelism here, the meaning of the proverb is skillfully two-fold. "The mind of the discerning acquires knowledge, and the ear of the wise seeks it." In this proverb, two kinds of people are labeled: the "discerning" and the "wise." The discerning man acquires knowledge. He listens and learns what is true. He knows things and retains those things. He is able to philosophically, intellectually and/or hypothetically test claims and discern between what is true and what is false, what is beneficial and what is harmful. He is a gainer and retainer of true information. But the man who is "wise" in this proverb takes action. He "seeks" knowledge. The wise man does not wait for knowledge to find him. He searches for it, acquires it and applies it. One who is merely knowledgeable is a situational opportunist against ignorance. But one who is wise is proactive.

Wisdom is not merely having knowledge, but what you do with the knowledge you have. I heard a story once about an experienced truck driver who got his 18-wheeler stuck under a bridge. The bridge's height was mislabeled by a couple of inches so he was working off of false information when he decided to drive under it. He knew everything about his truck and studied the available information carefully. But because his information was wrong, his truck was wedged tightly between the roadway and the bridge. Seeing the problem, a local police officer parked his patrol car and got out to help the driver think through a solution. They considered the potential dangers of backing out. They called an engineer to help them evaluate the possibility of jacking up the bridge a few inches from the middle, capitalizing on its built-in expansion joints. They combined their collective knowledge and experience to come up with the safest solution. A young boy was walking up from the distance. He studied the situation carefully as he approached. The same information was available to him as was available to the seasoned truck driver, experienced policeman and decorated engineer. Truck too tall. Bridge too short. That about summed it up.

The boy stopped to overhear the adults' conversation. After only a few seconds he made a move. While the professionals were collaborating, the young boy walked up to the truck and used his pocketknife to let the air out of the tires one by one. He approached the adults, tapped the truck driver on the shoulder and said, "I fixed it. Pull on through." And just like that the problem was solved. The adults may have been the most knowledgeable in this situation, but the boy was definitely the most wise. Knowledge is about what you know—however much or however little. Wisdom is about what you do with what you know—however much or however little.

Concerning going social, wise people incline their ears toward knowledge. Fools reject knowledge in favor of their opinions. Those who are wise hunger to know what is true so they can act on it in due time. The discerning/prudent are so labeled because their minds do the intellectual work of acquiring knowledge when the opportunity presents itself. But knowledge is not something a wise person merely stumbles upon by accident. It is something one should actively pursue with the resolve to apply. Paul told young Timothy, "Be diligent to present yourself to God as one approved, a worker who doesn't need to be ashamed, correctly teaching the word of truth," (2 Timothy 2:15). And to the Corinthians, "We demolish arguments and every proud thing that is raised up against the knowledge of God, and we take every thought captive to obey Christ," (2 Corinthians 10:4-5). It is impossible to be both ignorant and wise; knowledge is something we must pursue diligently if we are to live with wisdom. But it is very possible (and all too common) to be knowledgeable and foolish. Knowledge is something we must act upon appropriately, if we are to live with wisdom.

To be honest, it is mildly appealing to be intellectually lazy. If we can just hide within the confines of our own opinions and surround ourselves with people who agree with those opinions (or at least will not challenge them), we do not have to stretch ourselves to learn. We can be content with what we know and unconcerned with what we don't know. But guess what? The world is full of people who do not hold your opinions. Going reclusive is intellectually lazy. Going social is intellectually stimulating.

Our world, fallen from grace, is full of competing truth claims. One who is wise will not acquiesce to the prevailing philosophical winds of the generation, and one who is not a slacker will seek out what is true. Seeking knowledge is an active, willful pursuit of the wise man or woman. And when intellectual exercise is required to discern between true and false, the mind of such a wise man or woman goes to work.

When you live in community, understand that every truth claim you hear will not be true. Learn to discern between what is true and what is not true. Don't give into the postmodern intellectual laziness of theological or moral relativism. Do the work. And when you have the information, appropriate it correctly. Do something with what you know. Along your social journey, don't be satisfied with getting to knowledge while stopping short of wisdom.

PRAYER

O Lord, incline my ear to what is true. Guard me against intellectual laziness. Give me the discernment of a diligent mind. And make me wise, acting on the knowledge I have acquired in its appropriate time.

JOURNAL

_____

_____

_____

_____

_____

_____

_____

_____

_____

_____

_____

_____

_____

_____

_____

_____

_____

_____

_____

_____

_____

_____

_____

_____

_____

16. Every Word a Gift

"A person's gift opens doors for him,
and brings him before the great."
Proverbs 18:16

Duleep Singh was thirteen years old when he reigned as the last Maharaja of the of the Indian Sikh Empire, immediately before its fall to the British Empire in 1849. Upon the Sikh's surrender, the young Maharaja gifted Queen Victoria with one of the most valuable gifts in human history: the famed 186-carat Koh-i-Noor diamond. Also called the "Mountain of Light," Hindu legend says this diamond was a gift to humanity from the sun-god Surya. Record of its possession can be traced back all the way to the early 14th Century, within the Mogul Empire. Since 1852 it has been on display in England, and has even been set in a British brooch and subsequently in two different royal crowns. Today, it is on display at the Tower of London. Even at today's trimmed and refined size of 105.6-carats, the value of the Koh-i-Noor diamond is thought to be utterly inestimable. It is undoubtedly one of the most extravagant gifts ever given.

You and I will most likely never have the opportunity to even see this rare beauty, much less to hold it or to receive it as a gift. But can you imagine the extravagance?! What a gift! Everyone likes to receive good gifts. Regardless the reason for your visit, a good gift given breaks down barriers and opens up doors. You don't need to give someone a 186-carat diamond. Most of the time, it is the simplest gift given with loving thoughtfulness that means the most. Even in contemporary marketing classes students will learn that "I have something I'd like to tell you," is not nearly as effective as "I have something I'd like to give you."

Solomon, the wise king and author of this ancient proverb, was well accustomed to its truthfulness. The king is busy and often inaccessible to common folk. But those who brought a good gift found an open door. The verse reads, "opens doors for him," but literally translates, "makes room for him." The king made room for gift-givers in his busy schedule. Even the greatest of men and women are honored by a simple gift. And a simple, thoughtful gift unlocks and opens up doors that may be otherwise off limits.

This does not only apply physically, but conversationally as well. The way you speak to people can communicate either that you have something to tell them or that you have something you'd like to give them. Paul, in Ephesians 4:29, instructs the Christian that his or her words are to "give grace to those who hear." "Grace" in Greek (*charis*) literally means "gift." The words that come from our mouths should be giving good gifts to their hearers.

When our words are immediately and consistently offensive or proud, doors are shut and roads to the hearts of our hearers are blocked. What is your initial reaction when someone says, "I have something you need to hear," or "Let me tell you what you need to do?" How does that initial reaction differ from when they open the conversation with something like, "I love the shirt you're wearing today," or "The way you interact with your children really inspires me?" Which conversation starters would grab your attention more quickly? Which would find you more likely to make room in your busy schedule to hear what the other person has to say? When our words are gracious—gift-giving—to the hearer, doors are open and roads are paved into the listener's heart.

Do not confuse gift-giving words with empty flattery, however. The gifts our words bring are to be true and good gifts, or they are no gifts at all.

The Greek Philosopher Theophrastus, successor to Aristotle in the Athens school articulated it like this: "One may define flattery as a base companionship which is most advantageous to the flatterer." If the gifts you give are more to your advantage than to the receiver's, you are more of a user than a giver. Empty flattery designed to emotionally manipulate the listener is what is in view here. Instead, the idea is to cultivate a lifestyle of genuine graciousness so that appreciation of others is something that flows naturally from your lips. When this becomes a lifestyle of genuine conversational gift-giving for you, you will find doors opened and pathways paved that you never would have thought possible.

This is a particularly helpful practice for conflict resolution or confrontation. If you begin the conversation by defining and explaining what the other party has done wrong, you have immediately erected walls between you and your hearer. But if you begin the conversation graciously, you may just have a chance. Here are two ways to consider starting a conversation that you know will be potentially confrontational.

- **One: if you have anything for which to apologize, lead with that.** By owning your own guilt at the start of the conversation, you are leveling the playing field before making your case. If you do not have anything for which to apologize, do not make something up—that is flattery, not gift-giving. However, it has been my experience that in most ongoing conflicts both parties have at least some measure of guilt to own. Own it and apologize from it at the start. You will find this can open doors rather quickly.

- **Two: start with something positive or thankful directed toward the other person.** In the heat of conflict or debate it is extremely easy to forget the good things you know or like about the other person. Our minds immediately jump to the negative. Slow down, cool down and lead with a genuine word of thanksgiving or a positive word of encouragement. In doing this, you will find that it is much easier for you to keep your cool through the conversation, and to speak sincerely and graciously into the hearer's life.

As a pastor and church leader for over eighteen years, I have come to believe that many of our problems come back to this—we just don't know how to talk to people. I am often amazed to sit in a room with a group of people who all agree on the basic fundamentals of an issue and all hope to see the same end result, but who cannot seem to come to an agreement on even the simplest of details. Their words are swords, clinking and clanking on the battlefields of each others' emotions. Selfish pride are their protective shields and snappy, hurtful shots are daggers in each others' sides. In the end, relationships lay slain on the ground and not one has advanced his or her cause.

Sharp words sever good relationships. Gracious words heal broken relationships. Can you imagine how your social life would change—both in person and online—if you appropriated this ancient wisdom in every conversation? To take your conversational life to the next level, start this today. Every word from your mouth should be a gift to the hearer. That does not mean you should shy away from truth, but rather, that the truth can always be delivered in a package of grace. Just give it a try today: every word a gift. And watch how this ancient wisdom will open doors for you and bring you before the great.

PRAYER

Lord, communication is itself a gift from you, In every moment today, give me the wisdom and the self-control to give gifts with my words to every hearer. Fill me with your grace, that I might make every word a gift.

JOURNAL

_____

_____

_____

_____

_____

_____

_____

_____

_____

_____

_____

_____

_____

_____

_____

_____

_____

_____

_____

_____

_____

_____

_____

_____

_____

17. Don't Jump to Conclusions

"The first to state his case seems right,
until another comes and cross-examines him."
Proverbs 18:17

Do you remember the TV series Matlock? The show launched on NBC two months before my 4th birthday and aired its final episode on ABC five days after my 13th. I remember being a squirrelly little munchkin curling up on the couch with my Mom and Dad when the early episodes played. And I remember rolling my eyes, begging them to turn the channel to something better when the final episodes were counting down (you know, something better like Saved By the Bell, Home Improvement, or The Fresh Prince of Bel-air. Ah, those were the days).

Ben Matlock (Andy Griffith) was the man, though. He acted all ditzy and out of touch, but the dude was a genius. When he stood up in the courtroom, he had this calm, collected way of digging confessions out of the most unlikely of criminals on the stand. He would lead them on in a string of seemingly unconnected questions, and then boom! He nailed them. Their story seemed solid, until Matlock started poking holes in it. You weren't going to get one past Ben Matlock. Even if everyone else—

judge, jury and attorneys—jumped to conclusions, Matlock was going to investigate, interrogate and cross-examine until the whole truth came out.

Aesop, the ancient Greek storyteller, and author of what are now known as *Aesop's Fables*, once wrote "every truth has two sides; it is as well to look at both, before we commit ourselves to either." How true. Ben Matlock knew there are two sides to every story. And he wasn't about to commit to one before listening to the other.

It is in our nature to jump to conclusions. We are easily and quickly swayed, especially when information or inferences pull on our heart strings or seem to justify or verify something we already assume to be true (or want to be true). The social media culture has expedited this tendency. Most of the time we come to a conclusion—an emotional one—without ever considering two sides to a story or argument. We quickly jump into a conversation, online or otherwise, with strongly-held opinions, without even caring about the facts.

When a headline pops up that justifies or verifies some preconceived determination, we long for our voices to be heard more than we long to hear the voices of the opposition. We like, share, tweet or comment our ill-informed convictions and refuse to be counseled or corrected. Our predisposition toward self-promotion is herein exposed. We will amass to ourselves yes-men who will agree with, or at least affirm, our opinions. We will oppose those who oppose us without ever hearing what they have to say. We would much rather affirm the assumptions of our friends than entertain the idea that there may be another side to the story.

It should be obvious that opinions are not to be quickly voiced. *Should* be. But this proverb goes one step further (or should I say one step shorter?) by calling for patience not just in opinion-voicing but also in opinion-conceiving. Don't be so quick to convince yourself of something, especially when you know the particular circumstance is a hot-button issue for you. When our emotions get ahead of our brains, danger is near. Instead, wait for all the necessary facts and details to be uncovered before coming down on one side or another. Discernment is a gift from God, but it is also a willful exercise of the spirit. Paul tells young Timothy, "The sins of some are obvious, going before them, but the sins of others appear later," (1 Timothy 5:24). It often takes time for the whole truth to come out.

Recently our nation has been ravaged by the ignorance of this ancient wisdom. In 2017 alone, police officers shot and killed nineteen unarmed African American men across the United States. That number was seventeen in 2016 and thirty-six in 2015. The #blacklivesmatter and #bluelivesmatter movements formed quickly as people across America jumped to a "side" within seconds after every shooting. (Just the idea that these two true hashtagged statements could be viewed as contradictory is testimony enough to the reality of our deeply seated problems; surely black lives do matter, and blue lives do, too.) On social media, the news media and in person conviction-holders immediately and pointedly staked claims. On both sides of every particular situation, people were inconsolable by evidence and facts that may have contradicted their positions. Simple reason would acknowledge that some of these shootings were pointless, tragic expressions of institutionalized racism. But simple reason would also acknowledge that others of them, while still tragic, were genuinely justifiable.

Social media gives an immediate platform to anyone and everyone. Everyone is an expert and everyone's voice is equal, or so we permit. Fools of any ethnicity would be less concerned with discovering facts and formulating an educated conviction, and more concerned with using the tragic deaths of real lives to advance their emotionally-charged preconceived opinions. But those who are wise know, "The first to state his case seems right until another comes and cross-examines him." (And by the way, there is only one race—the human race. White, Black, Brown, Yellow, Red, or green with purple polka dots… all human beings are created in the image of God and are equally loved and valued by him.)

It is not wrong to have opinions and convictions. It is also not wrong to voice them (in truth, with grace). But it is unwise to formulate and voice those opinions prematurely or to hold to them unwaveringly regardless of the evidence. No one likes to be proven wrong. In our culture of self-promotion, admitting one's wrongness is regretfully uncommon. So when we publically come down on a particular side of an argument or conflict too soon, our instincts are to manipulate or ignore truth claims that surface to the contrary of our initial reaction.

But we can do better. Going social is difficult when you realize that we all (including you) have emotionally-charged connections to both issues and people. Emotions are not to control us. We are to control our emotions. Be careful not to formulate opinions about things before you have all the facts. And if you have done so already, choose humility and repentance instead of a bull-dogged insistence on your opinion. In the words of US President John Adams, "Facts are stubborn things; and whatever may be our wishes, our inclinations, or the dictates of our passions, they cannot alter the state of facts and evidence." Whether the issue is on the national news or on the next-door neighbor's porch, "The first to state his case seems right, until another comes and cross-examines him."

I cannot stress strongly enough the importance of this principle as it applies to social media. Social media outlets have given us instant platforms for every conviction and opinion. But instant platforms are not beneficial when coupled with emotionally-charged instant opinions. Have the discernment to understand both sides of every story. And have the patience to refrain from posting or commenting on something before you can do so intelligently and with grace. Even then, consider whether or not your post or comment might be unnecessarily divisive, or altogether unbeneficial.

What do you say? Make the cyber-world a better place today. Take a page out of this playbook of ancient wisdom for your contemporary social interaction.

PRAYER

Father, give me the patience to hold my tongue from immediate reaction. Help me to own my emotions and control them. Give me the discernment to listen to all sides of an argument before making up my mind. Give me the grace to speak and write/post according to what is true and edifying at all times.

JOURNAL

_____

_____

_____

_____

_____

_____

_____

_____

_____

_____

_____

_____

_____

_____

_____

_____

_____

_____

_____

_____

_____

_____

_____

_____

18. Go With the Flow

"Casting the lot ends quarrels
and separates powerful opponents."
Proverbs 18:18

Rock—Paper—Scissors. Yep. As primitive as it may sound to you, this is the quintessential argument-ending mechanism in the Wolfe household. We have two teenage sons who usually get along pretty well. But occasionally they surprise us with the things over which they will argue. Small things. Petty things. Things they both know really don't matter at all. Ethan and Aaron are both very intelligent and very strong-willed, and each of them loves to be right (a trait I'm sure they have inherited from their mother, because they could not possibly have gotten it from me...). We've tried other things. You know like logic, reason and compromise. Those don't work. My boys are definitely "powerful opponents" when they want to be. So when it comes to a head and all else fails, we stop them in their tracks and settle it man to man, with a decisive game of Rock—Paper—Scissors. None of this two-out-of-three business. One and done. Winner takes all. That's how we roll.

Strong-willed opponents like my sons and others you know (not you of course, for surely you're not hard-headed like them) sometimes have difficulty knowing whether or not something is a hill on which to die. Casting a lot, flipping a coin or throwing down in a quick game of Rock-Paper-Scissors is a great equalizer. There is no partiality. No favoritism. There are times when a display of strength is the right thing to do. However, most often strong-willed "powerful opponents" are fighting over things that, when all is considered, don't matter much at all.

Perhaps we are to take a couple of lessons from this proverb.

- **First, a lesson in *losing*.** When a display of strength is necessarily called-for, that's fine. But when the issue at hand is a peripheral matter and no agreement can be reached, flip a coin and just go with the flow. Losing that argument may be the only way to keep a friend. Did you catch that? Sometimes you have to lose to win.

- **Second, a lesson in *humility*.** The flip of the coin equalizes all parties. There is no great man or small man while the coin flips in the air or when it touches the ground—just two men. This is much like the end of our days; when all is said and done there will be no great men and no small men—just men. Casting a lot can end quarrels not only because a decision is made, but also because all parties involved are equalized. Human to human. Just the way God made us.

Is God sovereign? Absolutely. Are we? Absolutely not. God is never surprised by the results of our assumed serendipities or our lamented misfortunes. He sees the end of every argument better than we see its beginning. Sometimes allowing the chips to fall where they may while trusting that God is in the details is the only way to move forward. And when that is true, it is always a lesson in genuine humility and simple faith.

The 2016 Democratic primary was an intense one. The race between Hillary Clinton and Bernie Sanders had split the Democratic Party literally in half within the state of Iowa. Iowa being a very important battleground for both primary candidate elections and general elections, especially in the year of a presidential race, all eyes were on the nation's third most agriculturally productive state. In six Iowa precincts the vote was split evenly between the two Democratic candidates. The tiebreaker in Iowa's Democratic Party's caucus guide? You guessed it. An old fashioned coin toss. In what has become known as the "Miracle Six," Hillary Clinton won all six of these coin tosses, in a row. The statistical probability of that happening is 1 in 64, or 1.6%. The closest vote within the Iowa Democratic caucus in over 40 years was decided by the flip of a coin. Well, six coins.

In October of 2001, England's cricket team experienced an encouraging victory against Zimbabwe, but their big game-win was secondary in the news. The more exciting news, picked up and reported by media outlets around the world, was that the beginning of this game marked the team's first win in the coin-toss after 12 straight losses! The statistical probability of losing a coin toss 12 straight times is 4000 to 1, or 0.025%. The cheers for the coin toss win at the beginning of the game that day were louder than the cheers for England's 210 to 206 victory at the end of the game.

When you live in community with others, it is safe to say that things do not always go as planned. In fact, some of the most meaningful experiences you will have this week are those you could never have put on your calendar. Those who are best prepared to go social are those who are willing to roll with the punches—to go with the flow. Most of the time they don't need a coin at all. They know which hills are worth dying on (relatively speaking, these are very few) and which are best left either unclaimed or surrendered. When strong, powerful wills butt heads, consider the cost of winning and the value of backing down. To win an insignificant argument while losing a friend is no win at all.

Again, sometimes it would just be completely irresponsible to flip a coin. If you are trying to decide whether or not your date should be your spouse, don't flip a coin. If you are trying to decide which church to plug your family into, don't flip a coin. If you are debating core doctrinal principles or key elements of the faith, don't flip a coin. Some things are worth sincere, healthy debate. Fighting for what is right, the right way, takes energy, humility, courage, time, integrity and self-control. And if you have spent too much of your time fighting over any-thing, you will not have what is needed to fight for the right-thing. Some things can be let go. Some things cannot. Pray for the discernment to know the difference.

Consider also that some arguments are not lost when they are merely tabled. Issues and circumstances that incite strong emotions in people and those that have deep roots in one person or another often take time to work through. Time is not always the enemy in a disagreement. Time sometimes gives both sides the ability to evaluate the claims of the other, research where necessary and look at an issue circumspectly. Disagreements do not have to separate friends. There is a way to disagree civilly. And there is a way to have an ongoing disagreement without having an ongoing quarrel. There is a way to hold people to account without holding them in contempt.

Our culture is not naturally conducive to this. Rather, we are prone to be primed and ready for fireworks at any given moment. But if you practice ancient wisdom, you can learn to dissolve the tension behind a disagreement by listening for understanding and choosing not to win a pointless argument at the cost of losing a valuable relationship.

I wonder how this proverb can be applied to your relationships today at work, at home, with friends and/or online. Going with the flow means having the courage to decide when winning an argument may not be the best option. Going with the flow means having the humility to admit that your way may be the best way but it is not necessarily the only way. Going with the flow means having the flexibility to recognize a change of flow in the conversation and to choose the moment over the mountain. Going with the flow is nothing new. Going with the flow means appropriating ancient wisdom in your contemporary relationships.

PRAYER

Lord, help me discern which arguments are hills on which to die and which are not. Help me know when to stand and fight and when to flip a coin and go with the flow. Teach me to value the relationship over the win.

JOURNAL

_____

_____

_____

_____

_____

_____

_____

_____

_____

_____

_____

_____

_____

_____

_____

_____

_____

_____

_____

_____

_____

_____

_____

_____

_____

_____

19. Win Hearts, Not Arguments

"An offended brother is harder to reach than a fortified city
and quarrels are like the bars of a fortress."
Proverbs 18:19

"Good morning, America. What shall we be offended by today?" This tongue-in-cheek question was written as newspaper headlines, blog titles, social media posts and more across the United States in 2016-17. In a conversation on America's contemporary love affair with hyper-sensitivity, Fox News anchor Brit Hume noted only a few years ago, "In America today, if your sensibilities are offended by something that has happened, you get an enormous amount of credibility and are taken very seriously." In other words, being offended is the new being intelligent. People would rather hear from your feelings than from your intellect. And people will identify with your feelings more quickly and more consistently than they will identify with your intellect. Being offended is popular because it is celebrated, and it is celebrated because it is popular. Circular reasoning? How dare you suggest such a thing. I'm offended.

I read a story recently from a waitress at an urban restaurant. She was sharing her personal experience about a couple that had come in to dine one evening. They appeared pleasant enough as they waited and smiled cordially as they were shown to their table. The waitress glanced their way as they sat down, noticing a sudden change in their dispositions. The woman pointed to the wall and the man turned his attention. They began to converse irritably among themselves. As the waitress made her way to their table they got up from their seat in a hurry and stormed toward the door. The young server caught them as they were walking out and asked, "Is everything okay?" The inconsolable customer replied sharply and loudly, so that everyone in the restaurant could hear: "We refuse to eat at a restaurant with a Rebel Flag hanging on the wall!" They turned back toward the door and resumed their exit. The confused waitress managed to answer, "Sir, that's an Australian Flag." But it was too late. They were already offended and stormed out the door.

"An offended brother is harder to reach than a fortified city," wrote the wise, ancient king. When someone is offended the adrenaline is pumping, the pride is swelling and the solutions are fleeting. When anger and irritation go up, reason and humility go down. As a pastoral counselor, at times I found myself sitting across the desk from two individuals who were so offended by each other and angry with each other that they did not hear themselves saying the same things. They literally would indicate the same desires, reiterate the same problems and suggest the same solutions. But they were too offended by each other to realize that they agreed on more than they disagreed and wanted the same solutions the same way. Sitting across the table mediating this kind of conflict is a bit like watching two year old twin boys argue over whether what they are wearing on their feet are flip flops or sandals. I believe one time I actually—accidentally—let the words come out of my mouth: Are you for real right now?

Being offended is a choice. That's right. It's your choice. You cannot control what other people say or what they do, but you can control how you react to it. You cannot control their words but you can control your emotions. Being offended is usually more appropriately replaced by genuinely pitying someone else, and working harder at communicating truth with grace. If they only knew how highly you thought of them, as an image-bearer of God. If they only knew that there is a better, more loving way to communicate. If they only had the self-control and the wisdom to reword that phrase or act differently, they would be taken seriously more often.

What a shame that some choose to offend instead of to bless. What a shame that others choose to be offended instead of to be sensible. When someone is so naïve, so prideful, so ignorant or so hateful to say or do something that gives offense, he or she is completely missing the joy of community that is found in grace-filled living. When someone is so short-sighted and so ungrounded to obstinately harbor offense he or she is also completely missing out on the joy of grace-filled living.

The proverb says that it is next to impossible to win over an offended brother. Continued, heated arguments only strengthen the calloused bars around an offended human heart. Often the best thing to do is to affirm your sincere love for the offended person and offer opportunities to discuss the issue whenever he or she is ready. Prayerfully, when emotional temperatures decrease his or her ability to listen and understand will increase.

A special word here on social media arguments. You may have a personal experience to counter what I am about to write, but in my own experiences this remains true: I have never seen an important, heated debate either won or lost on social media. I have not seen even one person admit defeat, change their position or genuinely concede an argument. What I have observed is pointless conflict, endless debate, inappropriate name-calling and perpetuated frustration.

I have not seen a Democrat turn Republican or a Republican turn Democrat, but I have seen long-time friendships irreconcilably broken because of harsh words and name-calling from both sides. I have not seen comment threads full of understanding and empathy, but I have seen isolation and fragmentation into groups of "friends" and "follows" that only serve to affirm one's opinions and fuel one's offense. "If you voted for Trump, unfriend me now." "If I see the #blacklivesmatter hash tag on your posts, I will block you in the blink of an eye." So we favor our offense and burn any bridges that might lead toward understanding. We build walls around our hearts and fortify them with arguments that we convince ourselves we are winning. When we engage in needless social warfare we drive our stakes, sharpen our swords and fortify our walls.

But ancient wisdom would tell us to build bridges, not barricades. It would instruct us in the ways of winning hearts instead of winning arguments. So what are we to do in a culture that is so easily offended?

- **ONE: Work hard that your words and actions do not unnecessarily offend someone.** If someone must be offended by you, make it as difficult as possible for them to get over your gracious, loving disposition in order to do so.
- **TWO: Before engaging an offended brother or sister, recognize the spiritual warfare involved.** God created us for community. Therefore, social warfare is spiritual warfare. Pray for God to soften his or her heart toward reconciliation.
- **THREE: Understand that quarrelling back and forth with an offended brother only strengthens the bars around the heart.** The point of a healthy disagreement is never to destroy a person or to humiliate them. If you cannot win the heart while winning the argument, you have won nothing at all.

Those who are inconsolably offended are prisoners of their own hearts. Hearts are not won with sharpened swords or stinging words. Hearts are not won through endless, heated debate. Hearts are won by selfless service, gentle spirits and grace-filled living. Speak what is true, but don't quarrel needlessly. Have convictions, but don't build walls. Learn the value of this ancient wisdom and you will begin to create and maintain healthy relationships at work, at home and at play both among those with whom you agree and among those with whom you disagree: win hearts, not arguments.

PRAYER

Dear God, by the work of your Holy Spirit give me the discernment to know when to make war and when to make peace with my words. Keep me from needlessly offending brothers and sisters, and guard my own heart against needless offense.

JOURNAL

_____

_____
_____
_____
_____
_____
_____
_____
_____
_____
_____
_____
_____
_____
_____
_____
_____
_____
_____
_____
_____
_____
_____
_____
_____
_____

20. You Are What You Eat

"From the fruit of a person's mouth his stomach is satisfied;
he is filled with the product of his lips."
Proverbs 18:20

What kind of food do you like to eat? My family is pretty adventurous. As long as the restaurant itself is clean, we will normally try just about anything. We like everything from steaks and potatoes to sushi and cucumbers. Vanessa is an excellent cook. She likes to try new recipes and to modify old ones. When our boys were very young, they never had a problem trying new foods and appreciating what she had made. Some kids refuse to eat anything except chicken and french-fries. Not our boys. They have eaten spicy crawfish, sushi, boiled peanuts, wild-game chili and everything between since they had enough teeth to chew. Aaron, our youngest, was the exemplary positivist when it came to Momma's cooking. He praised her new creations and complimented her on the flavors. When he didn't actually like something she had cooked, he would take a single small bite then say, "Mmmmmm Momma that's good! I like that! I'm done," and excuse himself from the table.

"If you'd just try it, I think you'd like it." Mom-isms. Don't lie—you've said it, too. Does your child ever psych himself or herself out of liking something before the food ever even makes it on the fork? "But I don't like it!" the little one protests. "You've never even tried it!" comes the rebuttal. No matter. As soon as the morsel hits the tongue the face cringes, the lips spit and the throat groans. No, he "didn't even get enough in his mouth to taste." I know, Mom. But you will not convince him of that. He has already decided that he does not like it, and he will not be satisfied. Chicken and french-fries it is. Or the ole stand-by Goldfish. Thank God for Goldfish.

When we share our lives with others, the words of our mouths produce something and we eat to fill ourselves of that produce. We learn to manipulate consonant and vowel sounds and to change the tone and inflection of our voices in such a way that something—or someone—is affected. Either desired outcomes are produced or we change our vocal expressions. The point is, we have already decided what will satisfy us and the words of our mouths are designed to produce the desired satisfaction. If social interaction is to change from unhealthy to healthy—foolish to wise— unrighteous to righteous—it's not just the words of our mouths that must change, but the desires of our hearts.

The question is, what brings you satisfaction? What fills you? The words of a man's mouth produce something. There is no taking it back. Once a word is spoken it is planted in the fertile soil of the hearer's heart and mind. There, it will bear fruit. Words of truth spoken in love bear righteous fruit. Therefore, those who are only satisfied by righteous fruit will speak accordingly, and the return on their verbal investments will fill them with righteousness. However, words of malice pride, envy, and anger bear unrighteous fruit. Therefore, those who are satisfied by unrighteousness will speak accordingly and the return on their verbal investments will fill them with unrighteousness. Either way, as the words are spoken so the stomach is satisfied. You are what you eat.

Why do some people speak so harshly all the time? Seriously! Every time they open their mouths it sounds like they're angry at something or someone. A compliment sounds like a rebuke and an encouragement sounds like a complaint. But for some reason they are satisfied with the product of their lips. "That's just the way I am," they console themselves with no intention to evaluate the effectiveness of their communication. Satisfaction comes to them when they have spoken their minds, not when they have been understood. Their satisfaction is in self-expression, and the words of their mouths fill their stomachs with self-gratification.

There are others, however, whose words are always gracious and kind, encouraging and uplifting. An older woman at a church where I served had this natural disposition about her. I never heard a negative word come out of her mouth. She did not lie and did not water down the truth. But even the most negative words from her mouth were so positively framed that it was difficult to tell the difference. She was the kind of woman who could probably—if she wanted to—find a way to tell you that you've got it all wrong and you're losing in life but you'd still walk away saying, "Thank you." Communication to her was not a method of self-expression aimed at self-gratification. It was a pathway to meaningful relationship aimed at others' edification. There are those who are so filled and satisfied by good things that the fruit their words produce are always dripping with grace and wisdom.

People speak an average of 15,000 words every day. If every word we speak was written down, we would each author a 200 page novel every four days. The question is, would anyone want to read yours? What would those public pages reveal about the secrets of your heart? If you read what you had written, would it bring you satisfaction or turn your stomach?

There is a direct connection between the satisfaction of the gut and the communication of the mouth. Whatever is true of the former comes out of the latter and whatever fruit is produced by the latter is to the satisfaction of the former. We all need to do some self-evaluation occasionally. Perhaps instead of just evaluating your words today, you could search deeper to evaluate what satisfies your stomach. Jesus said that the words coming from your mouth are being produced from the overflow of your heart (Luke 6:45). Whether what you say is calculated or extemporaneous, it is still a reflection of your heart. Every word that leaves your lips produces fruit of some kind. And when you really think about it, the reason those words left your mouth is because your gut promised you a return of satisfaction. You are what you eat and you eat what you say.

Ancient wisdom calls the reader to learn to be satisfied by what is righteous first, if he hopes to plant seeds of righteousness and reap a harvest of righteousness later.

- "As the deer longs for flowing streams, so I long for you, God. I thirst for God, the living God." Psalm 42:1-2.
- "Taste and see that the Lord is good." Psalm 34:8.

Ancient wisdom for contemporary relationships. Long for what is good and righteous. Acquire a taste for what is both pleasing to God and good for your fellow man. Then and only then will the fruit of your mouth plant crops and reap harvests that satisfy your soul with good things.

PRAYER

Father in heaven, help me to acquire a taste for what is righteous and good. Teach me to be satisfied with good things and to despise the fruits of unrighteousness. Today, let my words plant trees and bear fruits that satisfy the hunger of my soul and not the hunger of my flesh.

JOURNAL

_____

_____

_____

_____

_____

_____

_____

_____

_____

_____

_____

_____

_____

_____

_____

_____

_____

_____

_____

_____

_____

_____

_____

_____

_____

_____

21. Speak Life

"Death and life are in the power of the tongue;
and those who love it will eat its fruit."
Proverbs 18:21

"Okay. I'm almost there." These were the last words texted from 18-year old Conrad Roy III's phone before he committed suicide in his parked truck in July of 2014. He had just about talked himself out of it, but his 17-year old girlfriend Michelle Carter was carrying on a lengthy texting conversation with him during which she repeatedly encouraged Conrad to "go ahead and do it." She gave him step by step instructions for filling his parked vehicle with Carbon Monoxide, and said that would be the best way to kill himself. "It will take like 20 minutes," she wrote. "It's not a big deal."

As Conrad expressed concern about his parents possibly not understanding and maybe feeling guilty afterward, Michelle texted, "Everyone will be sad for a while but they will get over it and move on. They won't be in depression. I won't let that happen. They know how sad you are, and they know that you are doing this to be happy and I think they will understand and accept it." From the morning hours of July 12 until almost 7:00pm, Michelle carried on the conversation with her boyfriend.

She even spoke on the phone with him twice, for more than forty-five minutes. When he got out of the truck and tried to abort his mission, she encouraged him to get back in and finish it. "Always smile," her thumbs struck each letter with calculated deliberation. "And yeah, you just have to do it... tonight's the night. It's now or never." More texting. More doubt. More pressuring. "Okay. You can do this," Michelle texted. "Okay," Conrad responded. I'm almost there."

Massachusetts Juvenile Court Judge Lawrence Moniz found Michelle Carter guilty of involuntary manslaughter in June of 2017 and sentenced her to 15 months in prison. Her lawyer, Joseph Cataldo, argued that Michelle's messages were protected under the First Amendment's free speech language. Highly publicized by every major media outlet, Judge Moniz's decision split the entire nation into two opposing opinions: those who agreed with the ruling and those who did not. Some argue that her conviction makes texting a crime. Others spout that Conrad was responsible for his own death—his actions were those of his own volition. Who's right? My gut tells me the opinions of those reading this book are as divided as those who commented publically on the court's ruling.

No matter how you feel about this incident legally, it is absolutely a horrible tragedy both physically and morally. A young life was horrifically ended as Conrad Roy III became convinced that his only consolation would be a permanent solution to a temporary problem. But the overwhelming heartache that follows suicide teaches every survivor that this is really no solution at all. In a moment when young Michelle could have spoken words of life into her distraught boyfriend, she chose to speak death instead. Whether the courts should rule her guilty or innocent is not my bone to pick here. But it is beyond obvious that the words she spoke and typed that day lead to death, not life.

God has bequeathed great power to the human tongue: the power of life and death. The tongue can either be a tool to build or a weapon to destroy. Each spoken word a gift of life that brings life to the hearer and returns life to the deliverer. Or, a disease of death that produces death in the hearer and returns death to the deliverer.

"Death and life are in the power of the tongue, and those who love it will eat its fruit." Contrary to its popular misapplication, this verse of ancient Solomonic wisdom is not about speaking wishes into reality. This is not a name-it-and-claim-it, blab-it-and-grab-it, health-wealth-prosperity magical formula of spoken faith. Rather, this is about the power of language—spoken, written or otherwise communicated—to either produce/sustain something that is good or to murder it. A word of life resurrects dead friendships; a word of death compacts the dirt on top the grave. A word of life lifts broken spirits; a word of death squashes all hope. A word of life is a blessing to the hearer; a word of death is a curse to everyone.

"Consider how a small fire sets ablaze a large forest," wrote James the brother of Jesus (James 3:5-8) only nine-hundred years after King Solomon penned his words of ancient wisdom. "And the tongue is a fire… It stains the whole body, sets the course of life on fire, and is itself set on fire by hell."

Sunday October 8, 1871 the worst fire in North American history had destroyed over 3.7 million acres in Wisconsin and Michigan, destroyed more than 3,000 standing structures and claimed the lives of 1,382 human beings. In the wake of this tragedy, that day would be despairingly referred to as "the night America burned." The cause of this relentless, gargantuan disaster? Lumberjacks and natives of the land were burning stumps and small, discarded branches. With a little wind and a little less carefulness, what started as harmless flames quickly grew into an untamable, ravaging horror.

"No one can tame the tongue," James writes. "It is a restless evil, full of deadly poison."

It is a bit unsettling when you think about it, how quickly a simple, flaming word can become a deadly terror. In our anger, our anxiety or our frustration we spout out a few heated words with a sharpened tongue. And within minutes we have set an entire relationship ablaze. Have you ever spoken a word carelessly that ended up burning a relationship to the ground? I have. It happens so quickly when carelessness invades normality. There are those whose every relationship is continuously, recklessly ablaze because they cannot, or will not, learn to speak life instead of speaking death.

"Those who love it will eat its fruit." When we speak death, we like to think our words are mortifying the hearer. But the restless evil—poison— that such communication burns within our own hearts is just as deadly as the fire it sets ablaze in our hearer's ears. Raging fire is no respecter of persons. The fires we set to burn others always end up burning us as well.

Speaking life or death is a choice in every moment. As communicated in previous chapters, my emotions are my responsibility and your emotions are your responsibility. We must not react in anger, but rather in love, truth and grace. I have personally witnessed too many bridges burned, too many relationships terminated and too many families torn to pieces by the power of a word spoken in death. Thankfully, I have also seen faces lifted, brokenness mended and deep wounds healed by the power of a word spoken in life.

Words are powerful. Every. Single. One. And they cannot be taken back. Your words can set a heart ablaze with life-giving hope or they can burn one down with murderous cruelty. Every word should be calculated and carefully chosen that it may be a word of life leading to life and not a word of death leading to death.

PRAYER

Holy Spirit of God, capture my mind and capture my tongue that in the heat of every adverse moment I might speak words of life that return to me in life. Guard my tongue from the ways of death and destruction.

JOURNAL

_____

_____

_____

_____

_____

_____

_____

_____

_____

_____

_____

_____

_____

_____

_____

_____

_____

_____

_____

_____

_____

_____

_____

_____

_____

_____

_____

_____

22. Be Wholly Committed to Your Spouse

"He who finds a wife finds a good thing
and obtains favor from the Lord."
Proverbs 18:22

In the Garden of Eden God reflected on all that he had made and remarked, "It is good." Except when he made man. Upon initial reflection of his pinnacle creation God remarked, "It is not good for man to be alone," (Genesis 2:18). So from Adam, God made Eve. Then, looking upon the two of them in beautiful community, God said, "It is very good." God created man and woman together as co-image bearers because he knew, in his infinite wisdom, that it was good to do so. When Adam was given Eve for his wife, he was shown favor from God.

Do you realize that before God instituted governments, neighborhoods, schools, social circles or even the church, he instituted the family. Specifically, marriage. Marriage is the social building block upon which all other societal interaction is built. The way God designed marriage—between one man and one woman for one lifetime—was good. It was a gift of his favor to mankind. This is not to intimate that an unmarried man or woman is less of a person. Each individual human being is created in the image of God, and as such is infinitely valuable to God and to mankind.

The point is that marriage—the kind of marriage that God deems "good"—is a foundational element to social interaction. From good marriages come healthy home environments where children are reared in the "nurture and admonition of the Lord," (Ephesians 6:4). From good marriages come positive models of conflict resolution and lifetime commitment to another. From good marriages come cheerful laughter and tearful sorrow in their appropriate seasons. The good marriage models the good life. And the good life is ultimately the desire of everyone who goes social.

"You complete me," says Jerry to Dorothy in what is possibly the most popular—and simultaneously most nauseating—love quote in movie history. Good reviews. Bad theology. A man is not incomplete without a wife and a woman is not incomplete without a husband. Yet ancient wisdom still persists that "he who finds a wife finds a good thing and obtains favor from the Lord." Marriage God's way is good. In fact, it is "very good." Humans were created for community. And the building block of meaningful community is the meaningful marriage.

"What does this have to do with going social?" you may ask. I had an interesting conversation the other day with a gentleman who was explaining how married men and women who are open to extramarital affairs give off certain signals. Vanessa tells me that I am generally oblivious to these signals, and she is right. God has gifted my precious wife with a discernment that I do not possess and often do not understand. Vanessa can spot a subliminally suggestive smile or gesture from across the room, and I thank God she is wise enough to physically and verbally come to my rescue before I am forced to pull a Joseph and run for my life.

These signals are many, and are often unique to each individual. A looker's openness can be communicated through the way she provocatively crosses her legs, the muscles that suggestively pull a soft smile to the side of his face, the smoothened tone and upward inflection of her voice, or the gentle inward lean of his opened posture. If your conscious or subconscious intentions, as a married individual, are sending off signals of inappropriate interests, your social life will inevitably be characterized by unhealthy conversations, unhealthy interactions, unhealthy emotions and unhealthy relationships. In the words of the great 20th Century American lyrical philosopher Johnny Lee, you will be "looking for love in all the wrong places / looking for love in too many faces." Such a looker has forgotten that a committed spouse is a good gift from God. Such an emotionally unstable temptress has despised the genuine Christlike love of a self-sacrificing husband. Such a wandering husband has traded the favor of God for the favors of a forbidden woman.

What's the answer? How is a married man or woman to remain unstained by the temptations of a culture that sexualizes absolutely everything? How can someone stay true to the "good thing" that God has given, when going social guarantees sexual temptation around every corner?

Marketing agencies will tell you outright, "Sex sells." Driving down the highway this week, you can see sexualized advertisements for everything from travel agencies to oral surgery. But ancient wisdom tells us that sex is a sacred favor, a gift from God to be enjoyed within the boundaries of marriage. The married person's mind is a constant battleground for social warfare in a culture obsessed with sex.

The struggle is real between the good thing that God has given to humanity and the forbidden things with which evil allures us. The only answer is to tame both the mind and the heart to think upon and to desire the overwhelming favor of God more than the illusory favors of a forbidden relationship.

Man and woman compliment each other so beautifully, by design. In a marriage that honors God, emotional needs, physical needs, social needs and sexual needs are all met with satisfied compliment. Not perfectly, of course, because married people are real people with real problems, too. But generally, by design, meaningful marriage brings satisfaction. This is favor from the Lord. But when a married person begins to seek the favors of someone who is not his or her spouse, the favor of God is forfeited and the good thing God has given is disparaged. Married men and women who lose sight of the good thing God has given them trade the favors of God for the favors of a forbidden love interest. And when the favor of God is traded for the favors of evil, going social is more like going self-destructive. Sex becomes a god and God becomes an afterthought.

Developing and maintaining healthy relationships in a fallen world can prove difficult in any environment. You will find going social even more difficult when your relationships are clouded by the twisted, emotional love-interests of those who have not learned to find their greatest joy in the good things God has given them.

When your friend's words about his or her spouse turn negative, bring the conversation back to the favor that God has shown him or her in marriage. When you notice that someone else is sending sexual signals to you, as a married person, get out of there as quickly as possible. When your mind entertains fantasies outside the boundaries of your own marriage, take your thoughts captive to Christ and remind yourself that marriage is a gift—a favor—from God.

PRAYER

Father, keep my eyes, my mind, my hands, my feet and my heart from seeking the favors of a forbidden relationship. Fill me each day with the joyful contentment of the good thing you have given me in my spouse.

JOURNAL

_____

_____

_____

_____

_____

_____

_____

_____

_____

_____

_____

_____

_____

_____

_____

_____

_____

_____

_____

_____

_____

_____

_____

_____

_____

_____

_____

23. Abandon the Entitled Attitude

"The poor person pleads
but the rich one answers roughly."
Proverbs 18:23

"Johnny Football," they called him. I am an LSU Tigers fan, personally. But Texas A&M football has had its moments in the Wolfe house. When Johnny Manziel gripped the pigskin during his freshman year at Kyle Field, for example, it would have been foolish to deny the raw talent this young man possessed. In 2012, his freshman year at TAMU, Johnny Football completed 295 passes for 3,706 yards, with 68% accuracy. His laser-focused passing game coupled with his mobility behind the line and unique ability to see the field earned Manziel the Heisman Trophy that year—the first time this honor had ever been awarded to a freshman. In his sophomore year his stats continued to improve; in 2013 Manziel completed 300 passes for 4,114 yards, with 69.9% accuracy. He was amazing! This initial success landed Manziel a draft into the NFL the very next year. In 2014 the Cleveland Browns drafted Johnny Football as the 22nd overall pick. But his career in the NFL would be short lived.

Johnny let the money and the fame go to his head. He was addicted to alcohol, wild parties and fast women. His attitude went from grateful to entitled with the simple stroke of a pen. His social media posts got him in constant trouble and it did not take long for the whole world to see that Johnny was into the money more than he was into the game. He stepped on the field only 14 times in two seasons in the NFL before the Cleveland Browns decided he wasn't worth the trouble and cut him loose. No other NFL team would even take a chance on him. The money and the fame had changed Johnny, and not for the better.

This year, in 2018, Johnny Manziel reentered the football scene for the first time in two years as a quarterback in the 4-game Spring League in Austin, TX. "Back to Texas where it all started," Manziel tweeted. "Can't wait to get back on the field and show NFL scouts what I can do." At the time of my writing it has yet to be determined whether Johnny will see the green turf of an NFL field this fall. But from March 28 to April 14 this year during the Spring League games, he found himself in a much more humbled position than he had been before. Whereas before, he felt like the NFL owed him a chance, now he finds himself begging for one. If he is granted such an opportunity in the NFL again, I pray that Johnny Football will allow the humility of his currently impoverished state (occupationally impoverished, that is) to maintain this levelheaded attitude. I pray the riches and fame will not make him forget the debt he owes to the NCAA, the NFL and to football fans across the United States.

"The poor person pleads but the rich one answers roughly," wrote the wise king. Generally speaking, poverty tends to humble a man while riches tend to swell him with pride. I imagine King Solomon had seen this many times in his rule. When the poor came before him they requested with humility, employing persuasive language and presuming only upon the king's mercy. But when the rich approached his throne, they did so with demanding language and presuming upon their own privileged entitlement.

Riches themselves are not bad. Certainly every person who has been so blessed by the hand of the Heavenly Father should be grateful. It's not money itself that is the root of all evil, as many incorrectly quote the Bible's wisdom. But rather, that "the *love* of money is a root of all kinds of evil," (1 Timothy 6:10).

When one is committed to his or her riches above all else, he or she loves the wrong things. When you love the wrong things, you are committed to the wrong things. When you are committed to the wrong things, your relationships are defined by the wrong things. When your relationships are defined by the wrong things, going social is more of a nightmare than a dream come true. Going social is only healthy when you genuinely love people. And you can't genuinely love people if you love money more. It just doesn't work that way.

It is a strange truth that something as crude as a dollar sign can completely change the demeanor of a man. There are exceptions. Some who are rich are humble and gracious, and some who are impoverished are demanding and rude. But generally speaking, riches can lead to pride. Poverty can lead to lowliness. The issue at stake is not money versus poverty but rather, entitlement versus detriment. If the ancient wisdom is to help us develop and maintain healthy contemporary relationships, then let us seek the favor of our listener from a position of impoverished detriment rather than prideful entitlement. Rather than presuming upon the riches of our bank accounts, our fame, our experience or our positions, let's always presume upon the grace and mercy of the other.

It's not just money and riches. The prideful person can be prideful over many things. He or she can be rich in influence, rich in experience, rich in education, rich in talents, rich in technical skills and more. These things are good in themselves, but none gives a man or woman the right to answer roughly. No matter the size of one's wallet or ego, healthy social interaction pleads with the heart instead of making demands of it.

No matter who you are, you will not go through life without asking someone for something. That is part of the joy of living in community with others. Every person eventually finds himself or herself in need of something someone else has. And every person possesses something he or she should consider graciously giving to someone else.

If God really did create us for community, and ancient wisdom tells us that he did, then in some small way we belong to each other. We are "good" by ourselves, but we are "very good" together. In God's eyes, no one person is more important or less important than another. Riches and poverty are all equalized at the footstool of the Creator's throne. After all, what do any of us possess that is not on loan from the one who owns it all?

The Egyptians buried their wealthy dead in tombs full of gold and precious things believing they would take their wealth with them into the afterlife. Today we invade their final resting places, exhume their sarcophaguses and display those same riches in museums all over the world. Not a single gold coin made its way into the afterlife, only the soul of the man or woman. We all leave this world the way we entered it: presuming upon the grace and mercy of God. Why would we waste a moment of a single day presuming upon anything less?

As contemporary faith-based author Patrick Meagher wrote, "Some people are so poor, all they have is money." Can I tell you something that will change your life? Money is not your problem or your solution. You don't need less and you don't need just a little bit more. If money is at all in the mix of your problems, it's not the acquisition of it or the abuse of it that really matters. It's the love of it that will make or break you.

In going social, don't ever let the numbers in your bank account affect the way you talk to or treat people. Be gracious. Be kind. Be humble, knowing that (a) everything you possess is on loan to you from the one who created and owns it all and (b) you will take none of it with you when you stand before God to give an account.

PRAYER

Lord God, if I am to be rich make me rich in love and grace. Guard my tongue from prideful demands. Instead, teach me to speak from humility at all times, pleading with the hearts of my hearers.

JOURNAL

24. Choose Your Friends Wisely

"One with many friends may be harmed
but there is a friend who stays closer than a brother."
Proverbs 18:24

Isn't it interesting that Proverbs Chapter 18 begins with the appeal to make friends and ends with the warning to be careful in the breadth and depth of your friendships? Right now, Selena Gomez has 127 million followers on Instagram and follows only 284 of them. Beyoncé boasts 106 million followers on Instagram and follows—wait for it—0. Kim Kardashian? 103 million followers, following 113. I get multiple requests for friendships and follows every single day from people I don't even know—not Selena Gomez, Kim Kardashian or Beyoncé, just to be clear (not yet anyway). Many of them are individuals I have never and will never meet face-to-face. How many friends do you have? Yeah, but how many friends to you *really* have?

The other day I met someone at the office for the first time. He had just stopped in for a quick visit. A colleague asked, "Dr. Wolfe, you know Mr. Smith don't you?" Recognizing the awkwardness in my eyes, Mr. Smith said, "Yeah, we're friends on Facebook." Oh yeah, that's right—we're friends!

In our day of social media obsession, we celebrate friendships that are ten miles wide and two inches deep. How many friends do you have? How many followers? How many likes? How many shares? No doubt King Solomon shared the same struggles, only in a different context. He was the most popular man in the world at the time. 1 Kings Chapter 11 shows us how even the wisest man in the world, when corrupted by riches and popularity, can make broad interpersonal relationships to the detriment of his own good: "they turned his heart away," (v.3). Everyone wanted to be the king's friend, but most of them were only in the friendship for what they could get out of it. Reflecting on this trouble, King Solomon knew that there was only a small number of close friends whom he could trust with his life.

The solution was not to isolate himself; that would be contrary to the wisdom of verse one. Rather, King Solomon's solution was to DTR (Define The Relationship). Who were the general friends and who were the close ones? It's not wrong to have many friends, as long as you remember the one or two who are not in it for themselves—those who will "stay closer than a brother."

When we go social, it is within the community of our friendships that we become who we truly are (interpersonally, anyway). If our only friendships are wide and not deep, we will become broad people with surface-level friendships and surface-level ambitions. But if you can see through the crowd to find the few, you can become a deep friend with deeply meaningful influence.

It is around these friends that we are most comfortable being ourselves. We become open and vulnerable there. If we are completely open and vulnerable with a sea of people, we will most likely drown beneath the relentless waves of betrayal and anxiety. But everyone needs that one friend—or those two or three—that are "closer than a brother." These are the friends who you know always have your best interest in mind because you always have their best interest in mind, too. These are the friends you have given permission to tell you things about yourself you may not want to hear but need to hear, and among whom this is reciprocated by your permission to speak into their lives as well. Proverbs 27:6 says, "The wounds of a friend are trustworthy but the kisses of an enemy are excessive."

"One with many friends may be harmed," the king writes with words of ancient wisdom. He knows the truth of this proverb all too well. During a time of peace, Solomon empowered a young man named Jeroboam, whom the king thought was his friend. Ultimately, Jeroboam would strip 5/6 of the kingdom away from King Solomon's household. His many, broad friendships led to the ruin of his reputation and the destruction of his hard work. A broad friend became his sharp enemy.

"But there is a friend that stays closer than a brother." Adonijah, King Solomon's older brother, made a demeaning request of their mother—a request conceived in bitterness and delivered in insurrection. Solomon was livid. He sent Benaiah, who had previously been in charge of the royal bodyguard for King David (Solomon's father), to put Adonijah to death. When Joab, the general of the king's armies, heard the news he was fearful because he was a supporter of the king's brother. So Joab defected and fled to the tabernacle for sanctuary. Knowing Joab's loyalty to Adonijah and hearing the news of his fleeing, the king sent Benaiah to execute justice. Benaiah returned to the king for clarity, since Joab was literally hiding behind the altar inside the tabernacle. Upon confirmation, Benaiah went back and struck Joab down just as Solomon had requested. Seeing Benaiah's loyalty, trustworthiness and prudence, the king made him the new commander of Israel's armies. In Benaiah, King Solomon found a friend who stayed closer than a brother.

If you are looking for mindless yes-men who will affirm your every opinion and only tell you what you want to hear, you're not looking for a friend who will "stay closer than a brother." You are looking for the kind of friendships that are many. Take heed, for among them you will likely, at some point, be harmed.

The challenge in a sea of friendships is to find the one or two who will actually stay closer than a brother. Don't look for those who are quick to affirm your every opinion, but for those who have the humility and grace necessary to challenge you and sharpen you in healthy, respectful dialogue. Don't look for the ones who will merely comment on your post, "I'm praying for you," but for the ones who will actually pick up the phone and call you. Don't look for the ones who share your tweets but for the ones who share your life. Don't look for the ones who will just come to your defense, but for those who will come to your side.

The point is not to despise the sea of broad, surface-level friendships. Rather, the point is that only when you have the special few can you appropriately relate to the overwhelming many. Who are your friends? I mean, your real friends? Are you the friend to them that you expect they are to you? When you are around them, are you encouraging them as much as they are encouraging you? Are you invested in their lives the way they are invested in yours? Eventually, people will let you down. Even the close few. The difference is that those friends who stay closer than a brother have the relational equity necessary to work through seasons of disappointment, while those who do not will jump off of your bandwagon as quickly as they jumped on it.

PRAYER

Thank you, Heavenly Father, for my friends. Thank you for the wide circle you have given me, and for all of their support and encouragement. Thank you also for the special few who stick closer than a brother. Help me be the friend to them that they are to me.

JOURNAL

_____

_____

_____

_____

_____

_____

_____

_____

_____

_____

_____

_____

_____

_____

_____

_____

_____

_____

_____

_____

_____

_____

_____

_____

_____

_____

_____

_____

Conclusion

The fork has been around for thousands of years. The earliest archaeological evidences of cultures using forks as utensils for food are bedded in the excavations of cities and homes that date back to over 2,000 years BC. It's just a handle with a few prongs on it. But for over 4,000 years the basic design of the fork has not changed. Sure, forks today are made from different materials than they were millennia ago. They are ornamented differently, and they are stabbed into different kinds of foods. But for 4,000 years the fork has remained pan-cultural, pan-generational and pan-geographical. It is an ancient tool that finds itself embedded in every contemporary generation. As it turns out, no matter how you want to use it you just can't improve on the basic construction of the fork.

The Bible was written thousands of years ago by people who lived in completely different cultural contexts than me. How can ancient words have such a contemporary application? As it turns out, as long as men and women have lived in social contexts, the basic truths of social interaction have not changed at all. People are people, no matter where or when they live. I pray that the wisdom of Proverbs Chapter 18 has given you tools for contemporary cultural engagement that will be as beneficial to you as they have been to generations of people over thousands of years. All of these truths are God's truths. And all of them are at your disposal, toward developing and maintaining healthy relationships at home, at work, among friends and online. But like any other tool at one's disposal, these will not make any difference at all if you don't pick them up and use them. Acquiring timeless truth is knowledge. Appropriate application of timeless truth is wisdom. Choose both, and watch how this ancient wisdom will breathe new life into all of your contemporary relationships.

Afterword

Here it is—the best part of this book. In the Introduction I told you as much. And now the moment you've been waiting for. The afterword of this book is good news. It's the best news.

Whoever you are and whatever you bring with you to the pages of this book, you are loved by God. I mean totally, completely, relentlessly loved. No one in any of your social circles could ever love you the way God loves you. The Bible says that God took great care to form you uniquely and beautifully in your mother's womb. God made you and God doesn't make mistakes. All of your days are written in his book before a single one of them ever begins. Even when you feel completely inadequate and unlovable, God loves you and has a plan for your life that is so much better than anything you could ever dream up for yourself.

Whoever you are and whatever walk of life you've come from, you are beautiful by design and designed for a beautiful purpose. "Tony, you don't know the kinds of things I've done." It is true that I don't know the complexities and shameful secrets of your life. But God does, and he loves you just the same. "God cannot possibly love someone like me." If these are your thoughts, there is a part of this equation that you are misunderstanding—or more appropriately, it's the whole equation that you are misunderstanding. There is nothing you can ever do to make God love you any more and there is nothing you can ever do to make God love you any less. You see, God doesn't love you because of who you are. God loves you because of who he is. And that is good news.

In fact, God proved his love for you in a tangible, self-sacrificial way. None of us deserves to spend eternity in heaven with God. Can you imagine if God allowed someone as sinful as you or me into his eternal home in heaven? Within seconds we would contaminate heaven the way we have contaminated the earth, in our sinful rebellion and pride. But because of his relentless love for you and for me, God demonstrated his love by stepping down from heaven, clothing himself in flesh and taking on himself the just penalty of our sin.

Jesus Christ—Emmanuel, God with Us—lived the perfect, sinless life that you and I could never live. He died a horrible death on the cross of Calvary to pay the price for sin that you and I could never fully pay. He was buried in a borrowed tomb to take our sin to the pits of the grave, where you and I could never fully take it. And on the third day he rose up from the dead to seal the victory over sin, death and hell for everyone who believes offering them forgiveness from sin and an eternal home in heaven, an extravagant gift that you and I could never earn. That is good news. In fact, it is *the* good news.

Like any other gift, the gift God wants to give you must be received. How do I receive such a gift? By believing in the message and ministry of Jesus Christ, God the Son, then confessing your faith in him as Lord and Savior. You can do that right now. You can call on the name of Jesus. There is nothing in your way except your own pride. Chose humility right now, and call on the name of Jesus to save you from your sin and secure for you a home in Heaven. Then go tell somebody. Tell everybody. A gift this extravagant is one you need to share with the world.

The Bible can seem complicated to someone who is just beginning to read and believe it. But it's not really that complicated at all. On every page, in one way or another, God is revealing more of himself to you. He doesn't just want to be like one of your many friends. He wants to be the One who stays closer than a brother. Jesus said in John 17:3, "This is eternal life: that they may know you, the only true God, and the one whom you have sent— Jesus Christ." God isn't in this for the numbers. He's in it for the relationship. He created you with such great care for that purpose—to have an uncorrupted, eternal relationship with you. Why? Because he loves you.

The more you spend time with God, listening to what he has to say in the pages of the Bible and talking to him through the discipline of prayer, the more you will come to know the heart of the Heavenly Father. Find a good community of faith—a church—to plug into (I am partial to Southern

Baptist ones), and grow deeper in your walk with God as you grow wider in your understanding of the world in which you live.

That's it. That's the good news. It's the best news I have. Even better than the news that you can have meaningful, healthy horizontal relationships with the people around you is that you can have a meaningful, healthy vertical relationship with the God of the Ages. And if you let it, this good news will rock your world for all of eternity.

It's been thirty years since I gave my life to Jesus and I have not gotten over it yet. One day I'll walk and talk with him just like Adam and Eve did in the Garden of Eden before sin entered the picture. But until then I'll hold fast to the promise of faith that he gave to me when I made him my Lord and Savior. And I'll keep telling everyone I know this good news because although I'm not yet where I am headed, when I get where I'm going I want you to be there too.

About the Author

Tony is the Director of Pastor | Church Relations for the Southern Baptists of Texas Convention. He earned his Bachelor of Music from Lamar University, Master of Arts in Religion and Pastoral Counseling from Liberty Baptist Theological Seminary, and Doctorate in Educational Ministry and Leadership from Southwestern Baptist Theological Seminary. He has served in full time vocational ministry since 1999 in the roles of worship/media, Christian education, the pastorate and denominational service. He and his wife Vanessa were married in 2001 and have two sons, Ethan and Aaron, who enjoy serving alongside them in ministry. Tony is also the author of *Mile Markers: Stages of Growth Along the Journey toward Spiritual Maturity*, *A Deacon On Purpose: Four Biblical Essentials*, and *7 Things You Must Do to Be an Effective Small Group Leader*. He invites you to connect with him on his personal website (www.tonywolfe.net) or any of his social media platforms at @drtonywolfe.

61622985R00102

Made in the USA
Columbia, SC
29 June 2019